ARCHITECTURE 05

ARCHITECTURE 05

.THE GUIDE TO

THE RIBA AWARDS

TONY CHAPMAN

RIBA ✸

MERRELL
LONDON • NEW YORK

First published 2005 by Merrell Publishers Limited

Head office: 81 Southwark Street, London SE1 0HX
Telephone +44 (0)20 7928 8880
E-mail mail@merrellpublishers.com

New York office: 49 West 24th Street, 8th Floor, New York, NY 10010
Telephone +1 212 929 8344
E-mail info@merrellpublishersusa.com

www.merrellpublishers.com

PUBLISHER Hugh Merrell
EDITORIAL DIRECTOR Julian Honer
US DIRECTOR Joan Brookbank
MANAGING EDITOR Anthea Snow
PROJECT EDITOR Claire Chandler
JUNIOR EDITOR Helen Miles
ART DIRECTOR Nicola Bailey
DESIGNER Paul Shinn
PRODUCTION MANAGER Michelle Draycott
PRODUCTION CONTROLLER Sadie Butler
SALES AND MARKETING MANAGER Kim Cope
SALES AND MARKETING EXECUTIVE Nora Kamprath

British Library Cataloguing-in-Publication Data:
Architecture 05 : the guide to the RIBA awards
1.Architecture – Awards – Great Britain 2.Architecture – Europe – 21st century
I.Chapman, Tony II.Royal Institute of British Architects
720.9'4'09051
ISBN 1 85894 306 X

Produced by Merrell Publishers
Edited by Tom Neville
Designed by Claudia Schenk
Printed and bound by Butler & Tanner, Frome

CONTENTS

TEASPOONS AND TOWER BLOCKS

Choosing from a list as diverse as the 2005 Stirling shortlist was, for judge Joan Bakewell, like choosing between a teaspoon and a tower block. But that's what some fifty judges whom I've accompanied in the ten years of the Stirling Prize have had to do. In that time we've visited sixty-three buildings in five different countries. I've covered 45,000 kilometres – going more than round the world in ten years. Exhilaration and exhaustion have been ours in equal measure; despite the generosity of our sponsors over the years, we've never done things in executive-jet style; for us it's been more easyJet and charabanc.

In 2005 we had probably the nicest and possibly the oldest set of judges ever. Despite early starts and missed connections, they were still smiling at the end. And still arguing all the way back to Edinburgh for the final judging meeting. Just eighty hours into his presidency, Jack Pringle hit the ground running, chairing a jury that also included Piers Gough, who so self-effacingly and inaccurately describes his architecture as B-movie stuff; Isabel Allen, a veteran of three judging panels and this year unencumbered by new offspring; Joan Bakewell, star of BBC arts, current affairs and religious broadcasting; and Max Fordham, who more or less single-handedly reinvented M&E engineers as environmental engineers, upping their street cred considerably in the process.

We gathered at Heathrow for an Aer Lingus flight to Cork, European Capital of Culture, announced as such by some signs at the airport, some new street lights in the city centre and a thin programme of low-key cultural events, all in keeping with a charming, modest city, whose natural setting rivals that of San Francisco. Our destination was a gem: O'Donnell + Tuomey's Lewis Glucksman Gallery at University College. The rain battered down as we made our way through a sylvan campus and there it was, poking through the sodden trees, each storey climbing on the shoulders of the one below as if to gain ever-better views. We were greeted by Fiona Kearney and Mark Poland, respectively director and project manager. The goal of the project is to bring Cork citizens as well as visitors from the world over to the campus, but arriving soon after opening time on a wet Sunday afternoon we had the place to ourselves. However, this is a gallery that will work well no matter what the visitor numbers. The Stirling judges were as charmed by the contrasting spaces as previous judges had been. Piers thought he saw a lot of Stirling here – could this be the sort of thing he would have been turning out now had he lived? Quite possibly. Piers also saw here a sign of a change in the way that clients and architects relate to one another. 'We stood under that cantilever and we were stunned', he said. 'Architects are allowed to be poetic now. It's not just about the effective use of space, it's about all sorts of things that raise the spirits and make life more enjoyable.' And the Lewis Glucksman Gallery certainly did that for all the judges.

With our visit over and with the best of intentions – and by way of comparison – we took taxis into Cork to visit the city's Crawford Gallery, extended a few years ago by the Dutch architect with the rock-star looks, Erik van Egerat. He's better looking than his building: a plate-glass double-height wall that obliged the curators to build an ugly white box inside in which to hang and protect the art. O'Donnell + Tuomey, for all the windows in their gallery, win that contest hands down.

7 .TEASPOONS AND TOWER BLOCKS

The Crawford Gallery was closed anyway, so we were forced to adjourn to the pub for lunch and to watch the Gaelic football semi-final between two Ulster teams. Joan was spotted by a keen young journalist who wanted to know her views on Cork as Capital of Culture. She was as discreet about that as she was about the building that was the reason we were there. The check-in computer at the airport, however, was not so sharp, failing to recognize her and her married name. After a short flight to Edinburgh, more taxis whisked us into the city, despite the protestations of the driver that we hadn't a hope of getting there on this the official last night of the Festival. Half a million pounds' worth of fireworks marked our steady progress.

The following morning we were greeted at the Scottish Parliament by John Gibbons, the former chief architect for Scotland, who had the unenviable job of acting *in loco clientis*. The original client having died, his place had been taken by a multi-headed Hydra comprising politicians who were equally divided between those who were set against the project on grounds of cost and location, and those who would roll over and agree to every cost over-run. Added to this was a deceased architect whose architect widow had taken on the project and seen it as one of her roles to freeze the design at the moment of Miralles's death, leading to inevitable difficulties with RMJM, the partners in a joint venture. That anything emerged from this process, let alone a building that might win the Stirling Prize, was remarkable. Perhaps being an Englishman in Scotland for once helped: it set Gibbons aside from the politics and enabled him to see the job through. Once we'd negotiated security arrangements worthy of an international airport, put in place at the time of the G8 summit and unlikely to be relaxed in the foreseeable and uncertain future, our tour began. It's a highly seductive building, winning over sceptics through the quality of its craftsmanship as much as by the intricacy of its design, which took 40,000 drawings to realize. Miralles was famed for his changes of mind. The last thing Donald Dewar said to him was, 'No more changes, Enric.' To which the Catalan replied, 'I will not change a thing unless I can find a better way of doing it.' He never did, and neither did his successors. If architecture is frozen music, this is frozen architecture.

Kevin McCloud, Channel 4's devil's advocate, questioned the judges in the Chamber. Piers thought it 'a feast for the eyes and the emotions'. Isabel was one of those who was won over: 'Everything you think is a problem ends up being wonderful.' 'What about the windows covered with sticks?' Kevin wanted to know. 'Don't you find that superficial?' 'Which bits of Chartres do you find superficial?' retorted Piers. Less rhetorically, Jack thought, 'If you argue about sticks, you don't get the building. It's about a torrent of motifs.' This building makes poets of us all. Max, our environmental conscience, thought it ticked all the boxes, though, as he'd said elsewhere (Cork), 'I walked in there with my checklist and threw it away the moment I saw it.' Only Joan had reservations: 'It's certainly powerful, but I keep looking for somewhere I can find a moment's peace.' But she agreed it would help interest people in architecture, which is at least half the point of this prize.

The next day we were whisked round London and the south-east by our driver, Gerry, who's seen nearly as many Stirling contenders as I have. First stop was Fawood, an apparently rough-and-ready building that is actually very sophisticated. The judges' eyes lit up like those of children on Christmas morning – appropriately so as this is gift-wrapped architecture, a steel mesh hung with brightly coloured baubles. Although not to the taste of everyone – that is, not Piers – it particularly excited Jack. 'It's fantastic, it's fantastic', this generally sober man repeated. The cage prompts the question: is it a prison for children or a friendly shield to protect them from the horrors of paedophiles and vandals? The Stonebridge Estate has a certain notoriety, some of it unfair – any murder within a radius of 5 miles gets attributed by the tabloids to the place. Joan liked the psychological relation to the outside world afforded by the cage: 'I buy the transparency that makes it a part of the community.' Sitting inside a Mongolian yurt made in Cornwall and plonked inside the cage, the judges discussed the centre's achievements with clients Andrew McNulty and headteacher Sarah Neno: the building gives them grown-up choices; sickness and absenteeism have declined at the nursery since its relocation here; suddenly it is easy to recruit good staff.

This is pure Cedric Price, a fun palace for kids. Piers loved (as Cedric would have) the temporariness of it; he was less keen on the 'patronizing' use of colour, but then maybe Piers and Will, a bit like siblings, are unable always to see eye to eye. The use of sea containers also divided the jury. Yes, they are a bit more expensive, once they've been stripped and elegantly fitted out, than new Portakabins would have been, or even new free-standing structures, but haven't we all seen too many examples of Portakabins badly used in schools?

The heated conversation continued on the bus until overtaken by the inevitable mobile calls. Joan had plumbers to deal with; Piers was demonstrating his insouciant way with clients. 'I've been away in the south of France', he drawled. 'I'll get round to your building soon.' Jack was worrying about how to get back from Brighton for a client meeting that evening; he managed it, even fitting in a live *Channel 4 News* interview in between.

We arrived at Woking and McLaren, where we were greeted by boss Ron Dennis and coffee served by black-clad staff. 'Norman and I were born on the same day,' Ron said, by way of explaining the perfect match of architect and client, 'and we're both Gemini.' That's why, apparently, Norman had to hand the job on to his partner David Nelson. 'I approached this project as I approach my life,' he added, 'as a search for perfection.' Through Foster's he has achieved it. 'I can see control is quite an issue here', Jack mused aloud. Not least when it came to budget: 'It was costed at £139 million and it came out at £138 point something million.' Eat your heart out Scottish Parliament (though rumour has it, the final budget was several times that and not that far distant from that for the parliament). But quality is just as important as quantity. At one point, quite unconsciously, Ron started referring to quality surveyors instead of quantity surveyors. His need for control is also demonstrated in the elaborate systems in place to remove all traces of the outside world from the staff between the car parks and their work stations. (They must have been round with a dustpan and brush cleaning up after those of us who had not been through the procedures.)

Maybe it was worth it – Ron would happily do it himself if he thought it was going to win him the Stirling Prize, which was his fierce and stated determination: 'We want to win at everything, whether it's a race or this prize.' Even the tea and coffee are controlled: they are only allowed in the magnificent staff canteen overlooking the lake; elsewhere it's mineral water only. Ron has a bit of a thing about catering: he was so upset about the quality of the food on an executive jet he hired once that he set up a company to provide such firms with high-quality food; it now has an annual turnover of £7 million.

After lunch, it was on to Brighton and the Jubilee Library. To many this was the surprise on the shortlist, not least because it was built under the Private Finance Initiative. Our guided tour was led by the project manager who has been with the scheme since day one, Katharine Pearce, the lynchpin all the more in PFI schemes, and by Sally McMahon, the librarian. She is looking forward to the day twenty-five years hence when the contractors who built and will run it hand the library over to the city and it will all be hers. But it's not on the list just because the quality is so remarkable for a PFI project – this could be a library for an extremely well-endowed university – but because it's also highly sustainable. When I came as one of the judges at an earlier stage in the process, it was the hottest day of the year and it was positively chilly inside, so well was the natural cooling working. No wonder, then, that it came within a whisker of winning our sustainability award.

Discipline was becoming a bit of problem towards the end of a long day. Trying to keep all the judges together to hear what was being said in library conditions was like herding prize cats. But I managed, and they were quietly impressed by the elegant spaces. Save for the mezzanines, it is one huge atrium with chimneys in the roof that draw the air through by a natural stack effect. Piers was full of praise: 'It's a very good building. Most architects don't understand buildings, they rely on service engineers. Rab really does understand buildings and makes sure they work.' Joan thought it showed a great commitment to the city, adding, 'The circulation is really well planned too.' Isabel had a carp about the cheap and almost randomly placed bookcases: 'The architects shouldn't have left it to the librarians. They have been allowed to ruin what is actually a very beautiful space.' And with its big fat white columns and almost sculpted ceilings, it really is beautiful.

On the final day we caught a much-delayed Lufthansa flight to Düsseldorf. 'The delay is due to appalling groundhandling at Heathrow', announced a buck-passing flight attendant. They certainly wouldn't be holding our connecting flight for Leipzig. But they did get us on to one to Frankfurt and from there to Leipzig, two and a half hours late. And although they didn't recognize Joan (unlike the Irish), at least one German recognized Isabel Allen, bumping her up to business class, leaving the rest of us, Kevin McCloud included, to slum it. *AJ* must be big there; *Grand Designs* obviously isn't. Kevin and I discussed the programme all the way there. I like his laconic style: he sells architecture with quiet enthusiasm and all the skill of a salesman who makes you desperate for something you never knew you needed.

At Frankfurt I had calls to make to rearrange our tour. The BMW manager and client, Peter Claussen, would not now be able to make it; we were in the hands of his PR. But this was a building that spoke for itself. And at least we got there, unlike Zaha, who sent her emissary, Lars Teichmann, the project architect, to talk to Kevin. The judges were bowled over by the Central Building. It links the two car-production sheds; the half-finished cars drift above the heads of office workers and diners in the canteen, where a veritable Clapham Junction of tracks comes together. This is a concept for which the client and architect fight to take the final credit – and why not? It's a brilliant one. Piers and I decided Zaha was a reincarnation of the Russian Constructivists. He also liked the changes in level – you move up and down a series of terraces – 'Zaha's ha-has', he called them. Joan was more taken with the *Marktplatz*, which, as well as being a place for the promotion of cars, doubles as a concert and dance venue. 'Great acoustics', she announced, clapping her hands. The others were applauding the building itself: 'the cathedral-like light' (Isabel); the curved glass on the façade 'like a windscreen' (Jack); its sustainable credentials – 'this is about as good as it gets' (Max); the quality of the concrete (everyone). 'This is diva architecture', Isabel told Kevin – well, someone had to.

We were discovering that it is difficult to get car-makers to talk about buildings. 'We turn out four hundred 3 Series a day,' Michael Janssen told us, 'soon to rise to 750 when we will have two shifts.' And he insisted on showing us the sheds, even though, sadly, the robots were on a tea break – no wonder the German economy's in a mess. Isabel noticed that the hangings for the tracks take the exact shape of the 3 Series. 'O brave new world that has such buildings in't', I exclaim, fortunately not to Kevin.

The judges now had seven weeks of purdah to mull over what they'd seen, during which time they were encouraged not to talk to one another. There was only one slight glitch: there was nearly no Stirling Prize to present, the X-ray machine and its minders at Heathrow having taken exception to the trophy in my bag. It didn't help that it looks like a Twin Tower. Still, it, and we, arrived safely to gather in a room at the Museum of Scotland in Edinburgh on the day of the presentation to choose between a couple of car plants, a cage for kids, ditto one for politicians, a stack of boxes for art and a glass box full of books. Piers certainly was keeping himself and everyone else guessing to the end: 'The great thing about having five judges is that your own choice may not necessarily win; therefore you get to talk about it, to discuss it, and in the end you may be persuaded to change your mind. The shortlist is so rich that I can easily imagine going into the room with one idea and coming out with another.'

So, which would you have chosen? The judges couldn't make up their minds. For two hours they batted the six buildings around before reducing the list to three: Cork, Leipzig and Edinburgh. So far so predictable. The next hour was tougher still, not least because there were only two and half hours to go before the start of the presentation. It was probably the hardest decision the Stirling judges have ever had to make; in most years any one of these buildings could have won. In the end the judges joined hands metaphorically round the table, closed their eyes and jumped. And the winner was …

11 .TEASPOONS AND TOWER BLOCKS

THE STIRLING PRIZE

IN ASSOCIATION WITH THE ARCHITECTS' JOURNAL

he RIBA Stirling Prize, now in its tenth year, is for the fifth year sponsored by *he Architects' Journal*. It is awarded to the architects of the building thought ⬤ be the most significant of the year for the evolution of architecture and the uilt environment. It is the UK's richest and most prestigious architectural rize. The winners receive a cheque for £20,000 and a trophy, which they old for one year.

he prize is named after the architect Sir James Stirling (1926–92), one of ⬤e most important British architects of his generation and a progressive ⬤inker and designer throughout his career. He is best known for his Leicester niversity Engineering Building (1959–63), the Staatsgalerie in Stuttgart ⬤977–84), and his posthumous Number One Poultry building in London. His ⬤rmer partner, Michael Wilford, won the 1997 Stirling Prize for the jointly esigned Stuttgart Music School, and in 2003 won a RIBA Award for ⬤e History Museum that completed Stirling's masterplan for the Stuttgart ⬤aatsgalerie complex.

his year's Stirling assessors were Jack Pringle, Joan Bakewell, Piers Gough, ⬤abel Allen and Max Fordham.

he winner of the 2005 RIBA Stirling Prize in association with *The Architects' ⬤urnal* was **THE SCOTTISH PARLIAMENT**.

THE SCOTTISH PARLIAMENT
.EDINBURGH .EMBT/RMJM LTD

The Scottish Parliament is a remarkable architectural statement. It has an enormous impact not only on visitors to the building but also on its users, who repeatedly move through a series of extraordinary spaces and their changing effects. That a project has outlived both its original client (Donald Dewar) and its architect (Enric Miralles) and still got built and built well, is very much down to the vision and dogged determination of one man: chief architect at the Scottish Executive, John Gibbons. This is his building every bit as much as it is Dewar's; just as it is RMJM's every bit as much as it is EMBT's. He was the man who had to ensure that the original vision of two men, who had achieved instant sainthood on their deaths and whose work could therefore not be touched, could be realized – and afforded.

The proof of the extraordinary architectural ambition and design vision is to be seen in every aspect and detail of the finished building. At the outset, Miralles made a major contribution in leading the clients towards a proper understanding of their needs and the final formulation of the role and function of the building. Further, through his awareness of the problems and knowledge of the subject, the architect has formulated the philosophy of the role of the parliament and reflected it in his architectural interpretation.

In its context the building manifests itself as an attempt at an organic transition between the city and the drama of the Scottish countryside surrounding it. The extremely successful landscaping makes this transition even more striking. The experience of the interiors is very impressive, and some of the spaces are real jewels in terms of internal public spaces (entrance hall, conference rooms and, above all, the Chamber). The list of admirable achievements in the building is a long one, and the ability of both the design and construction teams to realize a building of this complexity is truly remarkable.

The Stirling judges were almost unanimous in their praise for the building. Piers Gough was particularly short in dismissing the cost over-run question: 'It's only money, and governments spend idiotic amounts of money on things

CLIENT THE SCOTTISH PARLIAMENTARY CORPORATE BODY
STRUCTURAL ENGINEER ARUP
LANDSCAPE ARCHITECTS EMBT/RMJM LTD
BUILDING SERVICES ENGINEER RMJM SCOTLAND LTD
CONTRACTOR BOVIS LEND LEASE
GROSS INTERNAL AREA 29,321 SQUARE METRES
CONTRACT VALUE £250 MILLION
PHOTOGRAPHERS KEITH HUNTER/DUCCIO MALAGAMBA

in which I have no say.' Max Fordham agreed: 'All the best buildings have generous clients – it's difficult to create really great architecture on a shoestring.' John Gibbons, guide to the judges, explained the £200 million over-run in still more pragmatic terms: 'The £40 million original quote was a political figure – what Dewar knew he could get the politicians to agree. In fact he'd asked me what it would cost to repaint the old High School [an earlier proposed venue for the parliament] and quadrupled the answer. It was never realistic for a new building. What's more, the brief has changed out of all recognition: the first figure was for an 11,000-square-metre building, basically just a chamber; the MSPs' offices and so on take it to 33,000 square metres. Then there's the huge added cost of post-9/11 security.'

The Scottish Parliament is a once-in-a-lifetime building, and it is refreshing that, for once in the UK, a decision has been taken to spend a lot of money well, instead of an inadequate amount badly.

But this was about far more than money. Piers wanted to give the parliament the Stirling Prize for 'the genius of its urbanity'. And he summed it up with an oxymoron: 'Sophisticated politeness done with hysterical joy'. Fortunately he was a little more down to earth but even more passionate when interviewed live by Kevin McCloud after the announcement of its victory: 'The architectural profession has to dream … in the end the architect has to bring poetry … and that is the really important thing architects do, for God's sake, that's what we're here for, and that's what we must stick to; we mustn't be turned into monkeys working machines to build buildings. This is a passionate industry, where the architects bring to it poetry, beauty, magnificence and that's of course what the Scottish Parliament [has]. It's so fabulous. I mean, what a piece of landscape, what a beautiful interior, oh come, come on.' With which Kevin brought to a close the best (two-hour) coverage ever of the Stirling Prize.

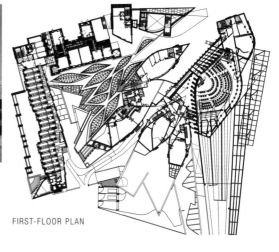

FIRST-FLOOR PLAN

BMW CENTRAL BUILDING AND PLANT
.LEIPZIG .GERMANY .ZAHA HADID ARCHITECTS

The Central Building is something of a rose between the thorns of two sheds, albeit one of concrete and one of glass. It is powerful but svelte – its form is a discrete sinew connecting to the blandness of the sheds that make up the rest of an efficient-looking car-production plant. Zaha's office and logistics building takes up just 26,000 of the 400,000 square metres (the area of fifty football pitches) of the whole plant, the rest of which was designed by the engineers for her building. It is almost coquettish in its allure, and it is only on entering under the flying concrete bridge into the enormous reception hall or *Marktplatz* – capable of holding 2000 people at the opening, but only a small part of what is in effect a single-volume building – that the extraordinary power of its vision is revealed.

Yes: you know immediately that car production is the central function, thanks to the nice conceit of half-finished Beamers gliding above your head on elevated conveyor tracks, making their silent, stately way between the body shop and the paint shop, weaving above 500 office and production staff. The embodiment of Zaha's sinuous, sensuous architecture, this is also dynamic, wholly fit for the purpose of a car plant.

Once the visitor's procession through the cavernous space begins, its functional organization becomes clear, as the separate functions intertwine and the visitor rises through the space on gentle inclines and steps connecting a series of mezzanines. Orientation is helped by colour-coded lighting – blue, for instance, indicates maintenance.

Circulation, offices and restaurants are barely delineated; and there are glimpses of cars being tested in the few fully enclosed – though only with glazing – spaces. (Instead of the 'them and us' mentality engendered by the design of most car plants, here office workers are involved in the process, even being encouraged in their lunch breaks to examine the minor faults thrown up by testing.) These are the endless variations of an evolving space. The experience is simply moving and breathtaking: powerful, serene and beautiful, all at the same time.

CLIENT BMW GROUP, MUNICH
PROJECT MANAGER ARGE PROJEKSTEUERUNG, ASSMANN-OBERMEYER
STRUCTURAL AND M&E ENGINEERS AGP ARGE GESAMTPLANUNG/ANTHONY HUNT ASSOCIATES
CONTRACTOR ARGE ROHBAU, WOLF & MÜLLER WITH OBAG
GROSS INTERNAL AREA 27,000 SQUARE METRES
CONTRACT VALUE €54 MILLION
PHOTOGRAPHERS HÉLÈNE BINET/MARTIN KLINDTWORTH

Even so, there is nothing gestural about this building. Everything is meticulously planned. It is built and detailed well, and it is clear from its commanding resolution that this radical form of a building has not just started here. It has been expanded and refined in the office and on smaller projects before cohering in this building: materiality, light, space, signage, doors, door handles, WCs, balustrades, the stuff of putting it together, all flow in one seamless space.

There were some concerns that the fit-out, designed by others – a quality office-furniture maker – did not live up to the architecture that it occupied, but, then, Zaha's building is a hard act to follow, and BMW insisted on using its regular interior architects. Nonetheless, this is a towering achievement by an architect – working again with her partner, Patrik Schumacher, and project architect, Lars Teichmann – who has finally fulfilled her enormous and much-vaunted potential. It is hard to do justice in words to architecture of this stature. Simply, it is a monumental building that works exquisitely on all levels. This architecture has arrived.

The Stirling judges enjoyed their visit from the moment they arrived and plunged under the concrete bridge into the cavernous reception area beyond. RIBA president Jack Pringle noted the car references: the flyover construction of that bridge to nowhere, the glass bonded on to the frames like a windscreen; but he also wanted to see it as a sperm whale. For him this was Zaha's chance at last to do an italic building after twenty years of drawing italic buildings, and Patrik Schumacher's opportunity to realize the office form he had lectured on for so long: the folded plates for offices that enable communication. A work of genius, which would have made a worthy winner.

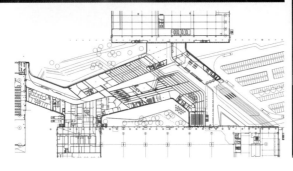

GROUND-FLOOR PLAN

FAWOOD CHILDREN'S CENTRE
.LONDON NW10 .ALSOP DESIGN LTD

The Fawood Children's Centre was commissioned by the Stonebridge Housing Action Trust to replace a nursery school. This is the initial step in a regeneration programme that will eventually see the centre overlooking new parkland. Currently it is squeezed in between Brutalist towers and slabs like a jewel in a tip.

As well as the facilities provided by the existing nursery school for three-to-five-year-olds, the brief included a small unit for children with special needs (mostly autism); the provision of space for adults' access to education; and a base for community education workers and consultation services. All this is in line with the government's Sure Start initiative for combining such facilities under one roof.

And this is quite a roof. The design concept addressed the requirements of internal and external space in an unusual but highly commendable way, by having the accommodation as freestanding elements within a larger enclosure. The three-storey-high accommodation is made from refurbished and adapted sea containers. Under a part-translucent, part-opaque pitched roof, the enclosure is made from stainless-steel mesh that incorporates coloured lozenges at the upper level, where the mesh adopts a series of waved profiles. The mesh, closer in weave near the ground and opening up as it rises, is only forbidding to those who should be forbidden. For the children it's rather fun. The resulting spaces between the cage and the containers accommodate different play areas and a yurt, one made not in Mongolia but in Cornwall.

Will Alsop is not perhaps an architect most obviously amenable to design-and-build contracts – he was novated to the contractor, Durkan – but the shotgun marriage seems to have worked well, with time allowed for architect and subcontractor to work on mock-ups of the steel mesh.

The RIBA Awards jury was particularly impressed by the concept of the 'friendly cage' enclosing functional and play areas. This device addresses the

CLIENT STONEBRIDGE HOUSING ACTION TRUST
STRUCTURAL ENGINEER ADAMS KARA TAYLOR
M&E ENGINEERS FULCRUM CONSULTING/ PINNACLE BUILDING SERVICES
CONTRACTOR DURKAN LTD
GROSS INTERNAL AREA 1220 SQUARE METRES
CONTRACT VALUE £2.3 MILLION
PHOTOGRAPHER RODERICK COYNE

sue of protecting children without depriving them of daylight and fresh air. ost nurseries solve the problem by placing outdoor play spaces to the ar of the building, enclosing them with far less elegant fencing than here. ut they are generally open to the elements and therefore of little use for rge parts of the year. At Fawood the philosophy is: keep the children dry d they'll keep warm by running around. The judges also liked the way in hich the cage is animated by the play of light on the coloured lozenges that ud the outer faces of the grille. And they admired the reuse of prefabricated xes (albeit fixed and immoveable) and the fact that the accommodation as multi-level rather than single-storey, adding further stimulus to the ildren's play.

e enthusiastic Head reported that her charges seemed to be considerably althier since the new building opened – a fine example of the beneficial fects of good architecture. She also reported that some of the older blings of the nursery attendees had commented that they wished they ere younger again. But there are two evenings a week of activities for older ildren at Fawood and the possibility of more to come. This is a nursery but so much, much more.

though the initial jury was bemused by the project when they arrived, ey left having been won over by its sheer bravado, carrying away pressions of amusement and delight. The Stirling jury also arrived without eat expectations but were quickly enthusing. Max Fordham was very taken th the cage: 'It could have been just a wire fence … It's marvellous that sop enabled that roof to be built, and the fact that you can't classify what indoor and what is outdoor space means that all those terrible acoustic gulations which are a straitjacket are turned upside down.' Joan thought e containers were 'Will being wilful', but otherwise she loved it. Jack had e final word, describing it as 'a mini-Peckham, a minor piece perhaps but very warm one. And at least you don't get taxi drivers hurling abuse as ey drive past, as they do at the Scottish Parliament.' But then of course u can't get a taxi driver to go anywhere near here.

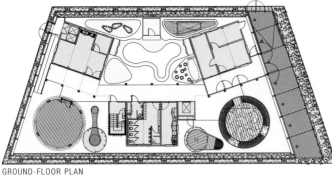

GROUND-FLOOR PLAN

JUBILEE LIBRARY .BRIGHTON .BENNETTS ASSOCIATES WITH LOMAX CASSIDY + EDWARDS

The library is the centrepiece of a regeneration scheme that stitches back together the fragmented streets of the North Laine area near Brighton's city centre. The developer cross-subsidized the building, a PFI project, with revenue from other developments. The library strikes a direct relationship with the square of which it occupies two sides, and it is clearly intended as a civic building of importance.

The developer of the site, Mill Group, approached local architects Lomax Cassidy + Edwards about the project – the library was part of a 1.75-hectare regeneration site and included seven other buildings. Nick Lomax decided to call on his former fellow Edinburgh students and friends Denise and Rab Bennetts. They won the OJEC competition as a joint venture. As is often the case in such situations, with planning permission gained the developer sold on the rest of the site, so the architects can see the pale shadows of seven of their proposed buildings rise around their library, but without their further input.

At least the library has stayed true to itself. The locally made blue tiles on the façade are a reference to the use elsewhere in the city of mathematical tiles. Otherwise it is largely glass-fronted; a simple, energy-efficient building with a good measure of style, as befits this swaggering seaside city. When the rest of the square is complete with its shops, hotel, offices and restaurants, a rundown quarter of Brighton will have been reinvigorated. The *Guardian*'s Jonathan Glancey has described is as 'a modest, potentially nourishing example of city-making that feels neither forced nor artificial'.

The glass façade is imposing, dissolving at night to expose the powerful library interior. The tiled entrance to the left of the main glazed façade is perhaps less perfectly resolved. But this is a building that is far more about its interiors. While the front elevations are somewhat – and deliberately – corporate, the internal volumes are warm and humane. The main library space is excellent. It has timber-clad side walls, fine concrete detailing and

CLIENT BRIGHTON & HOVE CITY COUNCIL
STRUCTURAL AND CIVIL ENGINEER SKM ANTHONY HUNT
SERVICES ENGINEER FULCRUM CONSULTING
LANDSCAPE ARCHITECT LAND USE CONSULTANTS
ARTISTS KATE MALONE/GEORGIA RUSSELL/CAROLINE BARTON
ACCESS CONSULTANT ALL CLEAR DESIGNS
CONTRACTOR ROK
GROSS INTERNAL AREA 6500 SQUARE METRES
CONTRACT VALUE £8 MILLION
PHOTOGRAPHER PETER COOK – VIEW

ALSO SHORTLISTED FOR THE RIBA SUSTAINABILITY AWARD

good natural lighting: it is both monumental and inviting. The massive white concrete columns rise to a vaulted ceiling; the effect is akin to that of being in a great Romanesque cathedral like Durham. It is a joy to be in.

The Jubilee Library was designed to achieve an 'excellent' BREEAM environmental rating, due in part to its low embodied energy, its low energy consumption and its use of recycled rainwater. The building has a clear and formal plan, with the environmental engineering clearly driving the structural expression. Thick concrete was used for the structure to help achieve thermal stability, with eight elegant freestanding concrete columns with fan-shaped heads supporting a middle floor and roof. Air is fed through voids in the concrete floorslabs to the perimeter rooms and the main space, with three centrally located wind towers that add to the skyline of a city known for its Regency domes and minarets.

There are many elements of the project to admire. Although, in the main, this is a one-volume space, different character is imparted to areas such as the children's library, the students' library and the AV collections – here the acoustic panels are so effective that it is impossible to hear the music being played until one enters the space. The library is enjoyed by both staff and user, and there is a strong public-art and exhibition programme.

Two nights before Stirling, the library picked up the prime minister's Better Public Building Award. A good omen perhaps, or a consolation prize (if winning an award the PM considers so important that he wanted to deliver it personally can be considered a runner-up prize)? For the Stirling judges, Jack said that he would be 'happy to resign as RIBA president now, if all public buildings were as good as this one'. Job done.

GROUND-FLOOR PLAN

LEWIS GLUCKSMAN GALLERY
.CORK .IRELAND .O'DONNELL + TUOMEY

The Lewis Glucksman Gallery is one of those buildings that can neither be captured in photographs nor properly summarized in words. Adolf Loos once said he was proud that his (and by implication other great) buildings could not be understood in photographs, and the same is true here. You need to visit it.

The building sits in a key position close to the entrance of University College Cork. On two sides it has a civic role in addressing the university and the city beyond; on the other two it has a completely different, almost picturesque, role in settling into an important mature landscape. That the building handles this difficult tension with apparent ease is the first mark of the incredible skill that the architects have brought to it.

In a way the architecture is full of contradictions: it uses everyday materials such as galvanized steel and MDF, yet it manages to appear luxurious (but not decadent); it has a truly astonishing cantilever, but it feels as if it should be there (rather than being a gestural shout); the walls of the gallery, which by tradition should be orthogonal, have bends in them, and they work; the building occupies the tight footprint of two previous tennis courts, but inside has a Tardis quality through the continuity of route and space; it employs none of the classical tropes for beauty, but looks astonishingly good; the galleries have a feeling of concentrated internality and yet one is always connected to the outside; the detailing is under complete control, but never fetishized. This is a rich and intellectually stimulating building.

To understand the experience one follows a *promenade architecturale*. This starts with one of the main routes of the university that cuts straight beneath the underbelly of the galleries. Le Corbusier used a similar trick, driving a major pedestrian route through the Carpenter Center at Harvard, but there the effect is to turn visitors into voyeurs; at Cork it democratically opens up the building to anyone. From the entrance one either descends (guided by a cold steel handrail) into the stone-clad, earthbound lower floors, apparently cut from the raw landscape, or rises (guided by warm timber) to the galleries

CLIENT UNIVERSITY COLLEGE CORK
STRUCTURAL ENGINEER HORGAN LYNCH CONSULTING ENGINEERS
M&E ENGINEER ARUP CONSULTING ENGINEERS
QS AKC CHARTERED SURVEYORS
CONTRACTOR P. J. HEGARTY & SONS
GROSS INTERNAL AREA 2295 SQUARE METRES
CONTRACT VALUE £7 MILLION
PHOTOGRAPHER DENNIS GILBERT – VIEW

above. Here one is nudged but not cajoled on a route upwards until at the top, just when one thinks one has reached a cul-de-sac and will have to retrace one's steps, a small staircase releases the tension and spins one back down. Along the route are incidents and placements that are beautifully judged, adding variety without being intrusive.

What is really remarkable about this building is that the more one looks, the better it gets. That is a sign of complete assurance and maturity. Miles Davis once said that what most artists do is to make simple things complex, but what great artists (and of course that included him) do is to make complex things appear simple. This is one of those rare buildings that fits that definition of great art. To cite two giants of the twentieth century in this report is not incidental. This building belongs to the canon of modern buildings.

Perhaps it was the romance of the visit, perhaps it was the Beamish, but afterwards Joan Bakewell thought she detected an architectural change: 'I think I can spot a certain return of sensuality generally to the feel of the places we have been to. They are softer, not quite as rigid, perhaps an emerging romantic strand in the way architecture is going.' Piers Gough thought it 'A Stirling building without the faults', though he did think Stirling's faults made his buildings more interesting. For Joan, the building gave her 'pleasure at every turn'; and Isabel liked the informal relationship of the building and the art and the way 'things can be small and heroic at the same time'. Piers was also moved to make a more general point about architects and clients: 'There's a generosity among clients towards architects. Architects are no longer the feared, frightening people who go and spend your money badly. There is a sense in which architects are allowed their freedom and this is what I mean by poetry.' The Lewis Glucksman Gallery has poetry in stanzas.

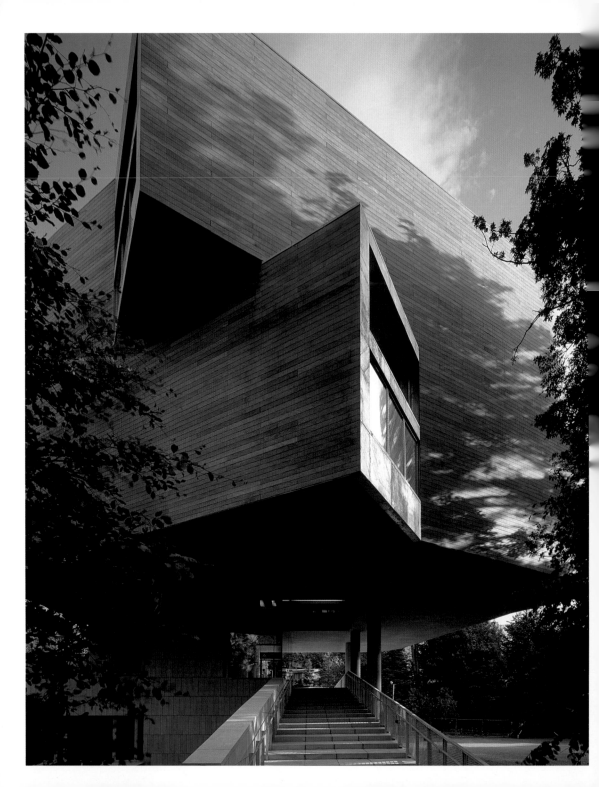

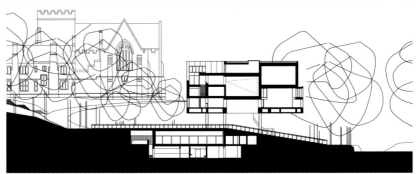

PLAN AND SECTION

MCLAREN TECHNOLOGY CENTRE
.WOKING .FOSTER AND PARTNERS

This new headquarters building on a 50-hectare site accommodates design studios, laboratories, research testing facilities, electronic development, machine shops, prototyping and production facilities for the company's Formula 1 cars and the Mercedes-Benz SLR McLaren. A concealed visitor centre is located in a separate building, all but buried under a grassy knoll near the site entrance. This will house temporary exhibitions, educational facilities and a presentation theatre, and is linked by a subterranean route. Here cars are currently stored under well-tailored shrouds, but it will eventually house a linear exhibition.

You arrive at the building having travelled around the lake, in Norman Foster's words, 'as if driving up to a country house'. The experience is perhaps closer to the world of Arthur C. Clarke than that of Agatha Christie. At first concealed by undulating grass mounds, the curved glazed façade suddenly appears in view, standing alone except for its own reflection in the lake. The building symbolizes McLaren, constructed with great precision in a meeting of minds, the client and architect having the same aspirations. A symbiotic relationship also exists between McLaren and its suppliers: whether they be Schüco, which developed the glass façade with McLaren; Boss, which supplies the black T-shirts and jeans worn by all staff; or TAG Heuer, which keeps the time at the factory and on the track – all McLaren's partners not only benefit from having an award-winning building to showcase their work, they are also expected to contribute to and share in the success of the Formula 1 team.

The plan of the main building is roughly semicircular, the circle being completed by a newly created formal lake, an integral part of the building's cooling system. Reed beds are also used to manage surface-water drainage as part of the environmental strategy. The principal lakeside façade is a continuous curved glass wall, shaded by a cantilevered roof. Internally there is one main double-height boulevard, 200 metres long, where classic sports and racing cars are lined up like trophies in a glass cabinet (the trophies themselves are round the corner). The boulevard defines circulation and articulates the fingers of accommodation, which are separated by 6-metre-

CLIENT MCLAREN GROUP
PROJECT MANAGEMENT ARLINGTON SECURITIES
STRUCTURAL ENGINEER ARUP
SERVICES ENGINEER SCHMIDT REUTER PARTNER
QS DAVIS LANGDON
PLANNING AND LANDSCAPE TERENCE O'ROURKE PLC
ENVIRONMENTAL ENGINEERING WSP DEVELOPMENT
PLANNING SUPERVISOR INTEC MANAGEMENT
LIGHTING CONSULTANT CLAUDE R. ENGLE LIGHTING
LAKE CONSULTANT ATELIER DREISEITL
SERVICES CONTRACTOR AMEC
CONTRACTOR KIER BUILD LTD
GROSS INTERNAL AREA 63,000 SQUARE METRES
CONTRACT VALUE CONFIDENTIAL
PHOTOGRAPHERS NIGEL YOUNG/MCLAREN GROUP (PAGE 37, PAGE 39 BOTTOM)/ PAUL GRUNDY (OTHER IMAGES)

ide streets. On the ground floor are the production and storage areas, as well as the hospitality suites and a staff restaurant, which look out across the landscape; top-lit studios, offices and meeting rooms are at first-floor level; a basement accommodates technical areas.

The build quality is remarkable, with exemplary detailing. This is a mature and confident scheme, six years in the making. Every detail has been considered, from the structural glazing to bolt heads and artwork. Many areas are breathtaking and very impressive, and even the more soulless parts are enlivened by colourful glass art installations. David Nelson, the partner in charge of the project at Foster and Partners and an industrial designer rather than an architect by training, is impressed by an attention to detail that is rare in a client, rarer still in the construction industry. He says: 'It's a kind of thinking you don't normally get in architecture. McLaren's standards are so high. Compared to the manufacturing industry at this level, the construction industry is miles behind, and very crude in comparison.'

For the Stirling judges, Isabel Allen detected a common theme in a number of the shortlisted buildings, not least at McLaren: 'I think you can see in all the buildings an appreciation of what used to be thought of as wasted space. So in the Lewis Glucksman Gallery you could ask why so much space is given over to a staircase, with the nursery you've got the cage, with McLaren you've got that great street. It's not just about square metres, it's about volume and void and it's what makes these buildings great.' Jack, a self-confessed petrol-head, thought it 'the best car showroom in the world bar none', and also likened it to Fawood: 'It's got the same diagram – boxes divided by streets, with a wiggly curve to make the architecture.' Piers was the most visceral in his response: 'I wanted to get down on my hands and knees and lick the floor.' In the end, although all the judges agreed the building was near perfect, it failed to lick the floor with the other contenders. What the judges wanted was a bit more life: perhaps if the street was fuller … perhaps if there were boats on the lake … or even a few hundred yellow plastic ducks. Who says architects aren't human?

TYPICAL FLOOR PLAN

RIBA SPECIAL AWARDS

The RIBA Special Awards are chosen from RIBA Award winners. They are assessed by panels that include specialist judges in the various fields who pay further visits to the shortlisted buildings. These seven awards reflect the diversity of architecture and reward the wide variety of specialist skills involved in delivering good buildings.

THE ARCHITECTS' JOURNAL FIRST BUILDING AWARD

The Architects' Journal First Building Award, worth £5000, is given for an architect's first stand-alone building and is sponsored by *The Architects' Journal* with Robin Ellis Design & Construction. Previous winners have been Cedar House, Logiealmond, by Walker Architecture; Barnhouse, Highgate, by Sutherland Hussey Architects; No. 1 Centaur Street, London SE1, by de Rijke Marsh Morgan and, last year, In-Between, London N16, by Annalie Riches, Silvia Ullmayer and Barti Garibaldo.

The Architects' Journal, founded in 1895, is the premier paid-for UK architectural weekly. Robin Ellis Design & Construction, the award's co-sponsors, were responsible for key parts of the refurbishment of the RIBA's headquarters in Portland Place, London.

It takes courage for an architect to set up on his or her own after seven years' training, and often several more years in the relatively safe environment of a bigger practice. This award is for those who have made that break and proved they can do it on their own.

The award was judged by a panel comprising: Barrie Evans, buildings editor of *The Architects' Journal*, Robin Ellis of Robin Ellis Design & Construction, and Silvia Ullmayer, one of last year's winners. They visited: GAZZANO HOUSE, LONDON EC1, BY AMIN TAHA ARCHITECTS; STEALTH HOUSE, LONDON SE5, BY ROBERT DYE ASSOCIATES; AND SURE START, TAMWORTH, BY SJÖLANDER DA CRUZ ARCHITECTS

The winner was GAZZANO HOUSE.

GAZZANO HOUSE
.LONDON EC1 .AMIN TAHA ARCHITECTS

This new Clerkenwell commercial–residential block – a deli and café on the ground floor and five storeys of apartments above – is clad in eye-catching Cor-ten, the steel alloy that includes copper so that it rusts, forming a patina that protects the building. Its height, and in some respects its form, are suggested by the adjacent fire-station tower used to practise rescues.

It is possible to discuss this project from the point of view of its urban contribution or how it performs in the stylistic melting pot of Clerkenwell (which it does very well, in the judges' opinion), but it is its materiality that is most provocative. The first thing you notice is that audacious use of Cor-ten steel as a cladding material for a modest urban housing project. Audacious, because Cor-ten had a relatively short life in the 1970s as a material associated with upmarket mid-Alantic office buildings. It re-emerged in the mid-1990s as the material used by Ian Ritchie for his Stirling-shortlisted Crystal Palace Concert Platform, and by Ellis Williams for the entry box at Baltic, the Gateshead arts centre. But when compared to the fiery red of Waterhouse's Prudential Assurance building in Holborn and the present enthusiasm for terracotta cladding in many housing schemes, with its rather predictable large-scale jointing pattern, the use of rusty brown of Cor-ten could be said to be an unlikely but interesting choice. Unlike the terracotta option, the surface of the building rather than the jointing system is emphasized. This allows the use of vertical and horizontal windows with some welcome large areas of blankness to form the principal compositional idea of this urbane elevation.

It is interesting to note that while architectural effort frequently goes into the flat plans, often resulting in rather ordinary façades, here this arrangement is reversed. One resident was critical of the hospital-white interiors, done by other hands. The sole internal point of interest is the use of oversized lettering in the common hall, reassuring visitors that they are indeed entering Gazzano House. Overall the judges thought that Gazzano House makes a definite architectural contribution to Clerkenwell's mix of styles and is a worthy RIBA Award winner for a young practice.

CLIENTS SOLIDBAU + JOE GAZZANO
STRUCTURAL ENGINEER ADAMS KARA TAYLOR
QS AND PROJECT MANAGER JACKSON COLES
M&E ENGINEER PETER DEER AND ASSOCIATES
CONTRACTOR TOLENT
GROSS INTERNAL AREA 1120 SQUARE METRES
CONTRACT VALUE £1.85 MILLION
PHOTOGRAPHER NICHOLAS GUTTRIDGE

The unanimous view of the AJ First Building Award judges was that all the shortlisted schemes showed architects delivering the finest architectural service to their clients and building users.

The judges said: 'Gazzano House won the jury over with its tough urban presence. It is a project where the skilful and robust conception survived the potentially emasculating rigours of changing briefs and dramatic budget cuts to emerge as a proud, contemporary and yet remarkably sympathetic addition to our urban landscape. This powerful six-storey volume now forms part of Clerkenwell's busy and varied streetscape of mostly brick façades dating from Victorian to contemporary times. It occupies a corner site and does this in a forthright, robust manner. Its rusting, weathered surfaces are contemporary on one level, while their grittiness and ability to age succeed in this typical London context.'

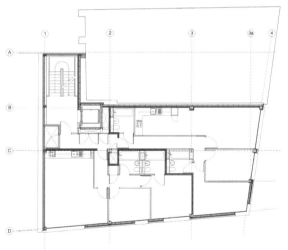

TYPICAL FLOOR PLAN

THE CROWN ESTATE CONSERVATION AWARD
SUPPORTED BY THE CROWN ESTATE

The Crown Estate Conservation Award is made to the architects of the best
work of conservation that demonstrates successful restoration and/or
adaptation of an architecturally significant building. It carries a prize of
£5000. Previous winners have included Peter Inskip and Peter Jenkins for the
Temple of Concord and Victory, Stowe; Foster and Partners for the Reichstag,
Berlin, and the JC Decaux UK Headquarters, London; Rick Mather Architects
for the Dulwich Picture Gallery, London; Richard Murphy Architects with
Simpson Brown Architects for the Stirling Tolbooth; LDN Architects for
Newhailes House Conservation, Musselburgh and, last year, HOK International
for the King's Library at the British Museum, London.

The Crown Estate manages a large and uniquely diverse portfolio of land
and buildings across the UK. One of its primary concerns is to make historic
buildings suitable to the needs of today's users.

The award was judged by Richard Griffiths, conservation architect; David
Pickles, senior architect in the conservation department of English Heritage;
Roger Bright, chief executive of The Crown Estate; and Tony Chapman, the
RIBA's head of awards. They visited:
78–80 DERNGATE, NORTHAMPTON, BY JOHN MCASLAN + PARTNERS; THE GRANARY,
CROWMARSH BATTLE FARM, PRESTON CROWMARSH, BY SPRATLEY & WOODFIELD; IGHTHAM
MOTE, SEVENOAKS, BY STUART PAGE ARCHITECTS; AND ISOKON (LAWN ROAD) APARTMENTS,
LONDON NW3, BY AVANTI ARCHITECTS LTD.

The winner was ISOKON (LAWN ROAD) APARTMENTS.

ISOKON (LAWN ROAD) APARTMENTS
.LONDON NW3 .AVANTI ARCHITECTS LTD

'Iconic' is now an overused and misused word, but it is absolutely appropriate when applied to Wells Coates's Isokon. The building epitomized modern city living when first built, in 1934; now, after conservation, it is an example of co-operation and regeneration. The original apartment residents included leading figures in the arts: writers such as Agatha Christie (who compared its sleek lines to those of an ocean liner) and émigré architects from Nazi Germany, including Walter Gropius and Marcel Breuer (who designed the communal Isobar on the ground floor). Now most residents are key workers in shared ownership with a housing association.

The building, listed Grade I but poorly maintained, had become uninhabitable. The client and design team won a competition to conserve, renovate and regenerate the block, and acquired it from Camden Council in 2000.

A thorough understanding of the integrity of the original design has informed the manner in which the conservation of the building has incorporated the essential repairs and upgrading necessary to achieve the standards expected of a contemporary living space. The plan and organization of the building differs from the original only in respect of the old ground-floor restaurant. This has been reconfigured to provide four more flats – which was actually the 1932 use of this space before the Breuer makeover. The interiors of the flats employ either refurbished original fittings or (mainly) like-for-like materials replicating the originals, resulting in new flats that are in close sympathy with Wells Coates's design but also incorporate modern appliances. Necessary new work, for example to satisfy current regulations, interprets rather than simply replicates what was there before. The penthouse flat occupied by the Pritchards, the developer-client, incorporates original flooring and joinery.

This project is exemplary in its approach to conserving the fabric of one of the key buildings of the 1930s, while also ensuring that the accommodation it provides is fit for current and foreseeable purpose. And this is more or less the definition of a new term that may now enter the architectural lexicon: 'isokonic'.

CLIENTS NOTTING HILL HOME OWNERSHIP/THE ISOKON TRUST (EXHIBITION GALLERY)
STRUCTURAL ENGINEER ALAN CONISBEE ASSOCIATES
QS STACE
SERVICES ENGINEER MAX FORDHAM LLP
LANDSCAPE ARCHITECT HEATON ASSOCIATES
CLERK OF WORKS FISHERKING 2000
CONTRACTOR MAKERS UK LTD
GROSS INTERNAL AREA 1147 SQUARE METRES
CONTRACT VALUE £2.5 MILLION
PHOTOGRAPHERS NICHOLAS KANE/JOHN ALLEN/GRESHOFF

The Crown Estate Conservation Award judges said: 'This long-neglected icon of the British Modern Movement has been saved with an outstanding example of creative conservation securing a sustainable future for a Grade I building at risk. The outcome is deeply satisfying in the way current use is carefully married to the existing structure, avoiding any damaging changes to Wells Coates's 1934 creation. This has been achieved by a mix tenure in which twenty-five of the smaller flats are allocated exclusively key workers.

The client and design team have shown great sensitivity in adapting and upgrading the building to current standards of comfort, servicing, safety and security without compromising the integrity of the design. In less skilful hands the outcome could have been quite different. This sensitivity is amply demonstrated in the acute attention to detail informed by a thorough understanding of the building's significance and vulnerability. Attention to detail encompasses such diverse elements as door numerals, paint colours, ironmongery, positioning of additional safety rails and new boiler flues. The design of new kitchens, dressing rooms and bathrooms is equally impressive its close reworking of Coates's original designs while meeting the needs current users. The policy of simultaneous sympathetic re-creation and adaptation of the original designs in the flats is highly commendable, but so also is the quite different policy applied to other parts of the scheme: the painstaking repair of the original joinery in the penthouse and the re-erection an original kitchen and dressing room in the former garage, to which public access will occasionally be available. Our only slight regret was that economic necessity prevented the retention and restoration of one small flat a permanent exhibition.

The design team has also demonstrated its understanding of the technical issues associated with the building both in terms of the repair challenges it posed at the outset of the project and the building's vulnerability during its future maintenance cycle.'

.THE CROWN ESTATE CONSERVATION AWARD

LAWN ROAD IN THE 1930

THE MANSER MEDAL
SPONSORED BY VELUX IN ASSOCIATION WITH THE BEST OF BRITISH HOMES

All the RIBA Award-winning houses and major extensions in the UK were considered for this year's Manser Medal and four were shortlisted. They will be featured in *The Best of British Homes* and also in the Best of British Homes gallery showcase of award-winning homes at Interbuild 06.

The Manser Medal is awarded for the best one-off house designed by an architect in the UK. The award is judged by a panel including Michael Manser CBE, Past President of the RIBA; Meredith Bowles, architect, winner of the 2004 Manser Medal; Michael Hanson, editor, *The Best of British Homes*; and Tony Chapman, the RIBA's head of awards. They visited:
COBTUN HOUSE, WORCESTER, BY ASSOCIATED ARCHITECTS; OAK FARM 1, LIVERPOOL, BY SHED KM; PRIVATE HOUSE, HOVE, BY BBM SUSTAINABLE DESIGN LTD WITH MILK DESIGN; AND STEALTH HOUSE, LONDON SE5, BY ROBERT DYE ASSOCIATES.

The winner was STEALTH HOUSE.

STEALTH HOUSE
.LONDON SE5 .ROBERT DYE ASSOCIATES

Set in a challenging suburban environment, and apparently the kind of project encouraged by *Grand Designs*-type TV programmes, Stealth House skilfully manages to avoid the kind of architectural showing-off that can sometimes be encouraged by television.

This house is an *ad hoc* amalgam of fragments of pre-existing buildings and major new elements melded into a convincing whole. Similarly, it seems to have fused the contributions of a professional architect and that of a talented jack-of-all-trades client to create an obviously much-loved family house.

The core of Stealth House is a 1950s bomb-site infill house in an Edwardian street with none of the homogeneity of many south London streets. Here anything goes, and Stealth House takes its cue from a number of elements of its neighbours: black timber from the flats opposite, a window detail from the Deco-ish house next door. The original house has been framed in timber and wrapped in cloaks of horizontal or vertical black timber and horizontal/ diagonal grey-green mineralized roofing felt. (You have to see it.) The result repairs the street in a way the 1950s set-back house never attempted, sharing a building line with a conventional Edwardian semi and a simple, rendered flat-roofed box. It has also increased the volume dramatically, turning a two-bedroom into a five-bedroom house.

To the rear the house is all transparency, with views through sliding glass doors or picture windows on to a well-planted courtyard garden; to the front the views are partially obscured with windows of etched glass or turned through 90 degrees. This gives the master bedroom a zen-like quality, despite the occasional whoosh of south London traffic (considerably dampened by the double glazing).

This is a house for grown-ups (and one teenager): a downstairs loo is hidden in what looks like a cupboard, but upstairs the elegant bathroom is open to a dressing room. Spaces glide into one another seamlessly, taking the visitor on a spiralling route that ends on the sadly unusable roof terrace. Southwark

CLIENT PRIVATE
STRUCTURAL ENGINEER GREIG-LING
SERVICES ENGINEER CAMTECH
CONTRACTORS CLIENT SELF-BUILD/ MADDERN CONSTRUCTION LTD
GROSS INTERNAL AREA 200 SQUARE METRES
CONTRACT VALUE £260,000
PHOTOGRAPHERS SUE BARR/ROBERT DYE/ CHRIS TUBBS

ALSO SHORTLISTED FOR THE ARCHITECTS' JOURNAL FIRST BUILDING AWARD

anning Department is to be congratulated, not for that, but otherwise for
ot only allowing but actively encouraging this architect-assisted self-build
oject. Much of the design emerged on-site as the result of a dialogue
etween the cabinet-maker client and his writer wife, the highly skilled
ntractor and the architect whose first stand-alone building – remarkably –
is is. Both as a minor but by no means trivial work of architecture and
a result of that exceptional partnership, it is a model intervention in a
burban setting.

e Manser Medal judges said: 'The design makes much of a tight site,
d shows how good architects can turn an unpromising space into a real
light. It provides a lesson to suburban house builders in how to get much
ore than expected from a standard plot, and shows how a striking
ntemporary building can be appropriate to its context. The design of the
use is clever in the way that it takes advantage of what the site has to
fer, allowing views while preserving privacy; dissolving the corners to
ovide views down the street; and using sunlight to add another dimension
a small house.

is also playful and witty. "As found" materials trace the original house
ainst the finish of the new work. There is also delight in the plan where
oms suggest possibilities rather than dictate a single use.

e details are beautifully executed. It has obviously been a terrific
laboration between a self-builder and an architect, and shows that doing
ngs in a non-conventional way is not only possible, but can produce
ildings of quality without high cost.'

GROUND-FLOOR PLAN

THE RIBA/ARTS COUNCIL ENGLAND CLIENT OF THE YEAR

The RIBA set up the Client of the Year Award eight years ago to honour the key role that a good client plays in the creation of fine architecture. Good architecture needs clients with both faith and vision. Everyone has benefited from the taste and persistence of good clients, from the Medicis to the city of Manchester. Arts Council England once again supported the award, as it has done from the start. The prize is £5000, to be spent on a contemporary work of art by an artist working in Britain. In this way the prize supports good architects and good artists.

Architecture is a team effort, as amply demonstrated by previous winners: Roland Paoletti, who received the first award for the new Jubilee Line stations; the MCC for commissioning a series of fine buildings at Lord's Cricket Ground; the Foreign and Commonwealth Office for pulling off a series of iconic embassies around the world; the Molendinar Park Housing Association in Glasgow for its campus of buildings by a variety of Scottish architects; Urban Splash for its commitment both to design quality and the regeneration of Manchester and Liverpool, the City of Manchester for transforming its public realm with a wide range of post-IRA bomb projects and, last year, the Peabody Trust for its pioneering work in off-site construction, the realization of truly sustainable housing, and in particular its commissioning of RIBA Award-winning schemes at Raines Court, London, by Allford Hall Monaghan Morris, at Murray Grove, also in London, by Cartwright Pickard and BedZED, Wallington, by Bill Dunster Architects.

This year's award was judged by members of the RIBA's Award Group, which is chaired by architect Jeremy Till and includes both lay members and architects. They considered clients of this year's RIBA Award-winning schemes but took into account a track record of previous successful commissioning, particularly where this has led to earlier RIBA Awards.

The 2005 shortlist was:
THE DEPARTMENT FOR EDUCATION AND SKILLS for RIBA Award-winning initiatives: the Classroom of the Future and the City Academies Bexley and Mossbourne;

SHEFFIELD CITY COUNCIL for its part in delivering the Classroom of the Future and Longley Park Sixth Form College, Sheffield; GATESHEAD COUNCIL for Sage Gateshead, the Millennium Bridge, Baltic: Centre for Contemporary Art and the Angel of the North; and HAMPSHIRE COUNTY COUNCIL for the 2005 RIBA Award-winning Alton Library and for a series of innovative and influential schools over the decades.

The winner was GATESHEAD COUNCIL.

In recent years Gateshead Council has commissioned a series of major art and architecture projects, each of which has contributed to the regeneration of the town and each of which resulted from well-run competitions.

The achievement is symbolized by council leader Mick Henry, who has been inspirational in his championing of, first, Antony Gormley's Angel of the North, the giant sculpture that announces to visitors from the south by road and by rail that they have arrived somewhere very special; then Ellis Williams's Baltic: Centre for Contemporary Art, winner of an RIBA Award in 2003, which gave the North-East world-class gallery spaces for the first time; and Foster and Partners' Sage Gateshead – a 2005 RIBA Award winner and winner of the RIBA Inclusive Design Award – which provides the area with a performance venue to match its deeply rooted musical traditions. All this would have been a significant achievement, but of course Gateshead was also the client for the RIBA Stirling Prize-winning Millennium Bridge. This project has won worldwide acclaim, and has both literally and metaphorically united Gateshead and Newcastle; after centuries of rivalry, they joined forces in a bid to become European City of Culture. Gateshead has led the way, and is a worthy winner of the RIBA Client of the Year Award.

THE RIBA INCLUSIVE DESIGN AWARD
IN ASSOCIATION WITH THE CENTRE FOR ACCESSIBLE ENVIRONMENTS AND ALLGOOD

This award celebrates inclusivity in building design and encapsulates an important new design philosophy. The principles of inclusive design have been articulated as follows: inclusive design places people at the heart of the design process; acknowledges human diversity and difference; offers choice where a single design solution cannot accommodate all users; provides for flexibility in use; and aims to provide buildings that are safe, convenient, equitable and enjoyable to use by everyone, regardless of ability, age or gender.

The previous winner of the RIBA Inclusive Design Award was the City of Manchester Stadium, Manchester, by Arup Associates. Winners of the predecessor prize, the ADAPT Trust Access Award, were the Royal Academy of Dramatic Arts (RADA) in London, by Avery Associates; Dance Base, Edinburgh, by Murray Fraser Architects; and The Space, Dundee College, by Nicholl Russell Studios.

This year's award was judged by Sarah Langton-Lockton, chief executive of the Centre for Accessible Environments; Mike Hield, managing director of Allgood, the architectural ironmonger; and Tony Chapman, the RIBA's head of awards. They visited:
CLASSROOM OF THE FUTURE, MOSSBROOK SCHOOL, SHEFFIELD, BY SARAH WIGGLESWORTH ARCHITECTS; PETER JONES, LONDON SW1, BY JOHN MCASLAN + PARTNERS; THE SAGE GATESHEAD, BY FOSTER AND PARTNERS; AND WESTON ADVENTURE PLAYGROUND, SOUTHAMPTON, BY FINCH MACINTOSH ARCHITECTS.

The winner was THE SAGE GATESHEAD.

.THE RIBA INCLUSIVE DESIGN AWARD

THE SAGE GATESHEAD
.GATESHEAD .FOSTER AND PARTNERS

This is undoubtedly an important building that may gain significance in the future as something of a watershed in the development of digital-technology-facilitated design. Clearly much of the design energy and resources have gone into its shapely envelope: the question the jury therefore asked itself was, how did its form suit its purpose?

The layout of the building is easily legible and functions well, with front-of-house facing the Tyne and forming a promenade through the building, while the backstage spaces are level with the service road at the rear. All three halls are constructed to high standards and are well-finished, impressive spaces with high acoustic standards, Hall One to such a degree that it is of national significance.

The curvilinear shape results in soaring spaces that are immediately pleasing, although the internal surfaces of the envelope, with its expressed decking and conventional, though imaginatively shaped, structural components, are surprisingly industrial in character. This is relevant to the client's (and the architects') ambition to make this public space – a wide public concourse that runs through the building – both active and democratic. For such a large structure, the building sits in its context very successfully; it appears almost to ooze out over the south bank of the Tyne valley. Some of the jurors found the pattern of glazing and steel cladding slightly unresolved; however, this is a question of style rather than substance.

It is quite clear that this project is very important locally. Tynesiders and others from the North-East have taken the building to their hearts, as they have with both the nearby Baltic: Centre for Contemporary Art and the Millennium Bridge, and with the Angel of the North, down the road. It is for this grand vision and single-minded pursuit of excellence that Gateshead Council is this year's Client of the Year.

The Inclusive Design Award judges said: 'This is a significant building on a sumptuous site. The Sage Gateshead is a highly successful expression of the

CLIENT GATESHEAD METROPOLITAN BOROUGH COUNCIL
ACOUSTICS ARUP ACOUSTICS
VENUE CONSULTANCY ARUP
COMMUNICATIONS DESIGN ARUP COMMUNICATIONS
SPECIALIST ENGINEER BURO HAPPOLD
FIRE ENGINEERING ARUP FIRE
COST DAVIS LANGDON
STRUCTURAL AND SERVICES ENGINEER CONNELL MOTT MACDONALD
LANDSCAPE ARCHITECT MICHEL DESVIGNE
ACCESS CONSULTANT BURDUS ACCESS MANAGEMENT
THEATRE CONSULTANT THEATRE PROJECTS CONSULTANTS
SPECIALIST LIGHTING DESIGN EQUATION
LIFT DESIGN LERCH BATES
CONTRACTOR LAING O'ROURKE
GROSS INTERNAL AREA 20,000 SQUARE METRES
CONTRACT VALUE £70 MILLION
PHOTOGRAPHERS NIGEL YOUNG/RICHARD BRYANT – ARCAID

GATESHEAD COUNCIL. CLIENT OF THE YEAR

clusive-design objective, which is to create environments that offer choice
nd equality of experience for all users.

principal tenet of inclusive design is the placing of people at the heart of
e design process. In this instance, dialogue with users through the Sage
ateshead Access Panel was established at the outset, and the access
nsultant worked on the project from inception to completion. The impact of
is is tangible in the sensitivity of the building to its users, notwithstanding
scale and super-sized spaces.

he layout of the building is readily legible and functions well. Performance
aces of all three auditoria and the loading dock are on the same level,
oviding exemplary accessibility for people with mobility impairments and
suring a high level of operational flexibility. All three halls are well-
ished, gorgeous spaces with high acoustic standards (also an attribute
inclusive design) and infrared systems.

ifts are large and can be used for evacuation; they are also "intelligent"
facilitate communication with Possum systems. Visual differentiation
achieved by careful specification of lighting, surface finishes and
nmongery. There are 200 WC cubicles, of which 27 are unisex accessible
cilities. There are both adult-changing and baby-changing facilities and
me accessible WCs have an overhead hoist. The Children's Room includes
Cs for children and accompanying adults. There is a palpable commitment
extending accessibility and inclusion in the broadest sense, through ticket
icing, a shopmobility scheme, free performances and the opportunity for
e public to sit in on rehearsals. The access panel continues to be actively
volved in the day-to-day operation of the building.'

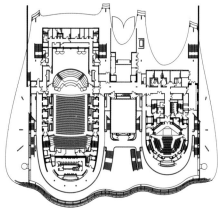

LEVEL 1 PLAN

67 .THE RIBA INCLUSIVE DESIGN AWARD

THE RIBA SUSTAINABILITY AWARD

This award is made to the building that demonstrates most elegantly and durably the principles of sustainable architecture. The prize was established in 2000 when the winner was Chetwood Associates' Sainsbury's at Greenwich. Subsequent winners have been Michael Hopkins and Partners' Jubilee Campus, University of Nottingham; the Cardboard School, Westborough Primary School, Westcliff-on-Sea by Cottrell + Vermeulen Architecture; BedZED by Bill Dunster Architects; and Stock Orchard Street, London N7, by Sarah Wigglesworth Architects.

This award was judged by a panel of experts including Bill Gething of Feilden Clegg Bradley, chair of the RIBA's sustainable futures committee; Bill Bordass, architect, of William Bordass Associates; Jeremy Till, chair of the RIBA Awards Group; and Tony Chapman, the RIBA's head of awards. They visited:

COBTUN HOUSE, WORCESTER, BY ASSOCIATED ARCHITECTS; CAMBRIDGE FEDERATION OF WOMEN'S INSTITUTES HEADQUARTERS, BY ELLISMILLER; JUBILEE LIBRARY, BRIGHTON, BY BENNETTS ASSOCIATES WITH LOMAX CASSIDY + EDWARDS; AND WESTON ADVENTURE PLAYGROUND, SOUTHAMPTON, BY FINCH MACINTOSH ARCHITECTS.

The winner was COBTUN HOUSE.

COBTUN HOUSE
.WORCESTER .ASSOCIATED ARCHITECTS

Cobtun House emerges seamlessly from the surrounding landscape. Approaching up an unmade suburban road, one is suddenly in the African bush. A curved mud and straw (cob) wall first encloses a series of south-facing sheltered terraces and then, with corrugated-iron roofs and oak-boarded walls, a sequence of beautiful daylit rooms. Each room is a surprise and each space has a fresh view of a landscape that has been skilfully crafted by the client. An expansive glass wall capitalizes on the unspoilt view across the Severn Valley and various *objets d'art* sprinkled throughout the house complement the architecture. The distinction between internal and external spaces is blurred, with the constant theme of tactile materials (mud, straw and timber) making both seem equally habitable.

Some of the technology may be primitive, but the architecture is refreshing and modern. This is a building that is truly sustainable but avoids wearing its green credentials on its sleeve. It was originally designed for a disabled client who required wheelchair access throughout, yet one is not aware of the array of apparatus that so often afflicts buildings designed for the disabled (although it is all there), even in the spectacular double-height shower room.

The architect's touch is light and playful, and the building successfully avoids being over-worthy or over-serious. It simultaneously draws from the technology of the middle ages and the twenty-first century to make a very sustainable package in terms of both embodied energy and energy in use. Its environmental credentials include the use of sun-dried clay from a nearby building site for the cob walls, saving on energy for transport and firing bricks; insulation made from recycled newspapers; internal joinery made from boards of compressed recycled plastic bottle tops; rain water that is harvested for washing machines, WCs and gardening; and hot water that is heated by solar collectors. The decision was made not to fit solar panels on economic grounds but provision was made for them to be retro-fitted.

The client's brief to the architect consisted of ten words: 'Humour, mystery and fantasy. Ecological, sustainable, independent. Contextual, agricultural,

CLIENT NICHOLAS WORSLEY QC
STRUCTURAL ENGINEER SHIRE CONSULTING
SERVICES AND ENVIRONMENTAL CONSULTANT LEDA
ENVIRONMENTAL BIOLOGIST CHRISTOPHER BETTS
COB WALL KEVIN MCCABE
CONTRACTOR G.F. HILL MALVERN LTD
GROSS INTERNAL AREA 246 SQUARE METRES
CONTRACT VALUE £255,000
PHOTOGRAPHER MARTINE HAMILTON-KNIGHT

ALSO SHORTLISTED FOR THE MANSER MEDAL

invisible'. The resulting house succeeds on every count. It is an outstanding example of what can be achieved when a client and architect work together with creative synergy.

The planning authority, Worcester City, shares the architect's and the client's enthusiasm for the project, using it in effect as a case study on its planning department's website. It writes: 'Cobtun House was originally part of the paddock and intensively used. A proposal was put together to build a single-storey house with environmentally friendly features, such as a green roof and a "cob" boundary wall made of straw and mud, with a requirement for the reintroduction of a wildflower meadow to the surrounding land that is in the Riverside Conservation Area. In giving the award the RIBA considered that the development "emerges seamlessly from the surrounding landscape".

'This view is shared by the City Council, which has previously granted a City Award for the development. It demonstrates that award-winning architecture can be sought in the city.'

The RIBA judges said: 'For sheer vision, the seamless and unobtrusive way the design was tailored to the client's needs, and the commitment and persistence of architect and client, the judges thought Cobtun House was a worthy winner of the RIBA Sustainability Award. Not only were some aspects of its construction truly innovative – particularly the use of materials such as earth, sand and aggregate from the site itself – the architect and the contractors so entered into the spirit of the job that they made a point of arriving on site by public transport or bike. The outcome is inspirational and not only pleases the client and his family and friends, it is also regularly visited by people keen to learn all about sustainable construction.'

THE STEPHEN LAWRENCE PRIZE
IN ASSOCIATION WITH THE MARCO GOLDSCHMIED FOUNDATION

The Stephen Lawrence Prize is sponsored by the Marco Goldschmied Foundation. It commemorates the teenager who was just setting out on the road to becoming an architect when he was murdered in 1993. It rewards the best examples of projects with a construction budget of less than £500,000. In addition to the £5000 prize money, Marco Goldschmied puts up an additional £10,000 to fund the Stephen Lawrence Scholarship at the Architectural Association in London, making this the second most valuable prize the RIBA makes.

The Stephen Lawrence Prize was set up in 1998 to draw attention to the Stephen Lawrence Trust, which assists young black students to study architecture, and to reward smaller projects and the creativity required when architects are working with low budgets.

The award was judged by architect Marco Goldschmied, Doreen Lawrence OBE, and journalist David Taylor. They visited:
ARTISTS' STUDIO, LONDON NW1, BY SANEI HOPKINS ARCHITECTS WITH HUGHES MEYER STUDIO; CLASSROOM OF THE FUTURE, MOSSBROOK SCHOOL, SHEFFIELD, BY SARAH WIGGLESWORTH ARCHITECTS; EXTENSION TO PRIVATE HOUSE, LONDON W1, BY HENNING STUMMEL ARCHITECTS LTD; HOUSE AT CLONAKILTY, COUNTY CORK, BY NIALL MCLAUGHLIN ARCHITECTS; AND THE ORANGERY, GREAT ORMOND STREET HOSPITAL, LONDON WC1, BY SPACELABUK.

The judges decided to give an unprecedented commendation to the Classroom of the Future because of its innovative use as a teaching tool, sensitive treatment of its lakeside setting, but perhaps most of all because of the measurable difference it has made to the schoolchildren's lessons and the grades they were achieving.

The winner was HOUSE AT CLONAKILTY.

HOUSE AT CLONAKILTY
.COUNTY CORK, IRELAND .NIALL MCLAUGHLIN
ARCHITECTS

Located in a small harbour looking north-east across Dirk Bay and sheltered by the Dundeady headland on the west coast of Ireland, an eighteenth-century cottage and a small complex of buildings associated with the boat slip for the old coastguard's station provided the genesis for this project. The architectural strategy was to design a building that made maximum use of its natural environment while remaining almost invisible from the public road skirting the bay. All the existing buildings were refurbished and the new, mainly glass and steel, extension is set against a thicket of mature trees that together form a boundary to the cottage.

The architect has responded brilliantly to the challenge of producing a building that would match the striking beauty of its site. Reference is made to 'beautiful shards of metamorphic rock that finger out to the sea from the base of the small cliffs'; the new building, which adds to the conversion of the boathouse and coastguard's cottage, produces a built shard of its own, distinctive but responsive to the geological forms around it.

Conversions are simple and effective, providing a master bedroom and bathroom in the cottage, and guestrooms in the boathouse. The new extension for living/dining is reached via a glazed cloister (a masterpiece of architectural understatement), the whole based round a quiet courtyard. The experience of each element of the design, from arrival to sitting at the dining table, is a journey in miniature, with powerful but not ubiquitous vistas of sea and coast complemented by domestic interior views. These range from the intimate whitewashed bedrooms in the old building to a glass-walled single-volume wedge-shaped living, kitchen and dining-room. The temptation to provide views from all points at all times has been wisely resisted, and the cliché of the big picture window in the extension has also been avoided in favour of a pair of separated framed views, one from the living area and one from the dining area immediately next to the courtyard.

Response to light has been a successful driver for the project, given that the relatively sheltered location of the existing buildings on a south-east-facing

CLIENTS EDWARD AND ANN FITZMAURICE
STRUCTURAL ENGINEER PACKMAN LUCAS STRUCTURAL DESIGNERS
LANDSCAPE CONSULTANT PETER FITZGERALD
MANAGING CONTRACTOR STEPHEN JEFFEREY
GROSS INTERNAL AREA 290 SQUARE METRES
CONTRACT VALUE € 500,000
PHOTOGRAPHERS NICHOLAS KANE/NIALL MCLAUGHLIN

site has resulted in a lack of sunlight. As the architect puts it: 'We have designed the extension to capture the last scraps of the sun as it declines behind the hill in the early evening'. The extension more than makes up for this, producing a totality in which comfort, aspect, light and geographical drama are synthesized to great effect. This is a mature building, the work of an architect with the confidence not to try to out-do his site but to complement it fittingly yet dramatically.

The Stephen Lawrence judges said: 'This stylish and accomplished private house extension is a worthy winner of this year's award in a strong field. The architect has exceeded the clients' expectations, delivering an intelligent and spacious project that maximizes light and connects and enhances the existing eighteenth- and nineteenth-century stone buildings on this stunning former coastguard site. It is also a testament to Niall McLaughlin's thoughtful skill and vision that the entire scheme sits naturally in its striking setting, avoids cliché, and successfully frames a series of delightful views with panache and élan. Ultimately, this is a housing project of enviable stature and a worthy yet subtle addition to a ruggedly beautiful – but unforgiving – coastal site.'

GROUND-FLOOR PLAN

THE RIBA AWARDS

The RIBA Awards were established in 1966 and, until the creation of the Stirling Prize in 1996, were made up of national and regional awards. Since then all the awards have been national but they are still judged by regional juries. They are first considered by a regional panel (and visited if there is any doubt as to whether they should progress further); the resulting shortlist is then visited by the regional jury, including an architect from the region, one from elsewhere and a 'lay' juror – engineer, client, contractor, artist, journalist, etc. The chairs of the fourteen regional juries then make their case for awards to the Awards Group (the scheme's advisory panel), which has the right to challenge their recommendations – and to query the ones they visited but did not recommend. If there is no agreement, members of the Awards Group have to pay another, what could be a third visit. And, still true to the principle that no project is rejected by people who have not seen it, they have the final say. The sixty to seventy confirmed awards are announced and celebrated at a dinner in June. From these winners, the shortlists for the Stirling Prize and all the other special awards are selected.

The assessors are listed in the following order: chair of jury (nationally appointed architect), lay assessor, regional representative
SCOTLAND Eva Jiricna, Mavis Cheek, Steven Spier
NORTHERN IRELAND Dipesh J. Patel, Joe Kerr, Clyde Markwell
NORTH-WEST Dick Cannon, Michael Dickson, Jonathan Davidson
NORTH Jim Eyre, Albert Williamson-Taylor, David Darbyshire
YORKSHIRE (no awards) Jim Eyre, Albert Williamson-Taylor, Gordon Carey
WALES Bryan Avery, Tom Dyckhoff, Alan Francis
WEST MIDLANDS John Pringle, Ed Glinert, Pam Newall
EAST MIDLANDS Peter Clegg, Laura Lee, Julian Marsh
EAST Laurie Chetwood, Julian Honer, Peter Goodwin
SOUTH-WEST Deborah Saunt, Adam Nicolson, John Taylor
WESSEX Deborah Saunt, Adam Nicolson, Peter King
SOUTH Bill Taylor, Felicity Goodey, Andrew Salter
SOUTH-EAST Paul Williams, Vivien Lovell, David Falla
LONDON EAST M.J. Long, Frances Morrell, Stephen Marshall
LONDON NORTH AND WEST Denise Bennetts, Alan Plater, Silvia Ullmayer
LONDON NORTH Isi Metzstein, Daphne Thissen, Paul Baker
EUROPEAN UNION AND WORLDWIDE Cany Ash, Emily Campbell, Tony Chapman, Paul Finch, Kathryn Findlay, Richard Griffiths, Glenn Howells, Louisa Hutton, Ed Jones, Tarla MacGabahnn, Niall McLaughlin, Eleni Makri, Paul Monaghan, Shane O'Toole, Alan Stanton, Jeremy Till

A'CHRANNAG .ROTHESAY .ISLE OF BUTE .G. DEVECI CHARTERED ARCHITECT

Built by the Argyll & Bute Housing Association to meet local needs for affordable housing and consisting of two- and three-bedroom homes for rent, A'Chrannag sits on one of the highest points on the Isle of Bute. The client had asked the architect for an innovative scheme on a beautiful site (previously occupied by an hotel), and one that respected the character of the landscape and the location's distinctive identity.

From the outset local participation was encouraged to create a sense of social inclusion and ownership. Local people selected a tower proposal rather than the blocks or terrace options, in order to minimize impact on the environment and landscape. The project has two flats on each floor with balconies and roof terraces for the top floors. The view from every apartment is breathtaking. The scheme also strikes the right balance between density and provision of green open space, and it develops an attractive design aesthetic of which the people of the place can feel proud.

A'Chrannag's sustainability profile is equally impressive. The building makes use of the best available technology for design to reduce waste and energy use; it makes a quantifiable contribution to greenhouse-gas reduction; it uses local human and physical resources to implement the development; it adopts best UK practice for sustainable development through partnering; and it maximizes public accessibility, especially for walkers and cyclists.

The judges visited one of the apartments belonging to a single mother. The quality of the environment and evident content of the occupiers was obvious and deeply touching. This successful collaboration, with an enlightened client working closely with the architect, fulfils a fundamental role for architecture: providing functional, comfortable shelter and facilities for people and their families without the means to buy or otherwise invest in property themselves.

CLIENT FYNE HOMES LTD
STRUCTURAL ENGINEER RAMAGE AND YOUNG
ENERGY CONSULTANT GÖKAY DEVECI
CONTRACTOR STEWART AND SHIELDS LTD
GROSS INTERNAL AREA 1200 SQUARE METRES
CONTRACT VALUE £1.5 MILLION
PHOTOGRAPHER ANDREW LEE

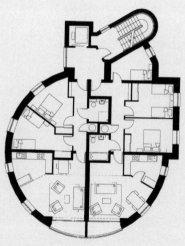

FLOOR PLAN

SENTINEL OFFICE DEVELOPMENT .GLASGOW .GORDON MURRAY AND ALAN DUNLOP ARCHITECTS

It is rare to find a speculative administration building that is both excellent and inventive. This Glasgow office development stands out. Situated on the corner of two relatively busy streets in the city's financial district, it caught the judges' attention initially at night, with its exterior lighting effects, and subsequently during the day as a very clean, simple building with a great deal of visibility and integrity.

Planning approval (initially subject to a maximum of five storeys) for this inexpensive ten-storey structure was cleverly obtained because of its careful composition: the elements of the building step in and out, creating different levels so that the adjacent development is not overshadowed and does not suffer any loss of natural light.

The façade is clad with Cumbrian slate panels in combination with an elegant structural-glazing system, consisting either of clear or translucent glass panels placed at random – a solution that gives the impression of discipline and a very highly controlled level of detail.

An innovative LED lighting system incorporated in the glass cladding allows the exterior of the building to go through various changes of colour, with impressive results. A fully glazed floating reception cube with a glowing LED light and sculpture arranged around one of the supports of the building is visible and recognizable both day and night. It is a building designed and built with skill, ambition and confidence – qualities that were maintained throughout the project.

CLIENT KENMORE PROPERTY GROUP LTD
PROJECT MANAGER CBA
STRUCTURAL ENGINEER HALCROW
M&E ENGINEER K.J. TAIT ENGINEERS
CONTRACTOR MILLER CONSTRUCTION LTD
QS THOMAS AND ADAMSON
GROSS INTERNAL AREA 8309 SQUARE METRES
CONTRACT VALUE £9.8 MILLION
PHOTOGRAPHER ANDREW LEE

PICAL FLOOR PLAN

FALLS LEISURE CENTRE
.BELFAST .KENNEDY FITZGERALD & ASSOCIATES

On a key site marking a peaceline between the Falls Road and the Shankill area, the Falls Leisure Centre is a critically important project in a series of regeneration initiatives on this major arterial route close to the city centre. Although initially lacking in detail, the brief was clear in its main objectives: a landmark building that addressed the issues of regeneration and low-energy use.

Previous leisure centres in Northern Ireland have been designed as impenetrable masonry fortresses. The Falls Leisure Centre is an heroic open building that is a clear symbol of the post-Good Friday Agreement age, both by day and by night. The courageous use of different coloured glass brings life to the street and welcomes the community in. Despite having been open for only three weeks when the judges visited, the building had already seen usage exceed expectations. At night it is a lantern of varying colours, and the amenity lighting has been cleverly used to obviate the need for street lighting around the building.

The centre has a legible plan and good daylighting in the main sporting spaces. Materials are robust and simply detailed. Provision has been made for several multipurpose community spaces that provide practical support to regeneration ambitions.

Even ignoring history and context, this is a building that sets new standards for leisure centres. It uses the available budget to great effect and creates a venue that draws in its community. Sport is recognized as a good way to promote health, build social capital and encourage social integration. The Falls Leisure Centre does all of this and looks set to be a regenerative flywheel in a location that has much need of such help.

CLIENT BELFAST CITY COUNCIL CLIENT SERVICES DEPARTMENT
PROJECT MANAGEMENT BELFAST CITY COUNCIL DEVELOPMENT DEPARTMENT
STRUCTURAL ENGINEER RPS KIRK MCCLURE MORTON
M&E ENGINEER WILLIAMS & SHAW
QS CYRIL SWEETT
CONTRACTOR GILBERT ASH (NI) LTD
GROSS INTERNAL AREA 4115 SQUARE METRES
CONTRACT VALUE £5.7 MILLION
PHOTOGRAPHER KENNEDY FITZGERALD & ASSOCIATES

KINNAIRD STREET OFFICE
.BELFAST .MACKEL & DOHERTY ARCHITECTS

This, the architects' own office, consists of three terraced houses, the first of which has been the practice's base for several years. Kinnard Street is a short terrace off the Antrim Road, with what was a park, now an army base, at one end. Once an affluent area, it is now partially derelict. The practice is successful and needed to grow, so it had two options: locate to new premises, or expand the existing office. To support the local community-regeneration project the architects decided to commit themselves to the area.

The street frontage is essentially unchanged. Only the purple paint, new doors and views through existing windows give clues to the dramatic transformation within. Internally, the original office is largely unchanged and now provides support accommodation to the new working spaces in the two other houses. The new spaces are formed as a set of connected volumes providing the equivalent of an open-plan working environment across two houses. In addition to use by the architects, space on the ground floor is available for the community to hold meetings and social events. This has its own front door and links to a courtyard garden to the rear.

For a modest budget the building provides a stimulating and modern working environment. Simple balustrade details are used to set the language of the interior and heighten the sense of interconnection between spaces.

Above all, the extraordinary achievement of this project is its contribution to the community and the urban setting. The houses across the street were scheduled for demolition, and it seems likely the same would have happened to the whole street had the architects relocated. Instead, leading by example, their project has inspired the Belfast Housing Executive to change policy and renovate the houses.

CLIENT MACKEL & DOHERTY ARCHITECTS
STRUCTURAL ENGINEER MARTIN WYNNE LAVERY LTD
SERVICES ENGINEER DR D. LAVELLE & ASSOCIATES
CONTRACTOR CANAVAN CONSTRUCTION
GROSS INTERNAL AREA 480 SQUARE METRES
CONTRACT VALUE £200,000
PHOTOGRAPHER MACKEL & DOHERTY ARCHITECTS

GROUND-FLOOR PLAN

31 BLACKFRIARS ROAD
.SALFORD .OMI ARCHITECTS

The old Manchester Baths is a Grade II listed building, its pool infilled in 1960 when the building was converted for light-industrial use. Now OMI Architects have converted it into four design studios, including one for their own office.

As well as specifying essential internal and external repairs, the brief was to make a series of design studios aimed at the creative industries and to play a positive role in the regeneration of a run-down part of the city. The result is simple and stylish, new and old forging interesting and unusual relationships. Despite a modest budget, the feel and appearance of quality in key areas has been achieved by the careful manipulation of space, material and detail.

The building is organized around an efficient, rational plan and an inventive section that places small voids in strategic locations, effectively exploiting light, volume and views of the existing roof structure. Floor heights have been deliberately varied to increase the sense of drama and to introduce varying levels of intimacy.

As you progress through the building there is an effective hierarchy of elements, detailed with skill and flair, that enriches the experience and provides much of the building's identity. The inclusion of a mezzanine gains additional floor space and is visually interesting in itself; however, the usable space is somewhat compromised by the existing trusses that prevent this feature from being fully exploited. This is an accomplished project achieved on a modest budget.

CLIENT OMI GROUP
STRUCTURAL ENGINEER ANTHONY HUNT ASSOCIATES
M&E ENGINEER BARRATT ELECTRICAL + MECHANICAL
CONTRACTOR HARRY NICHOLLS (BUILDERS) LTD
GROSS INTERNAL AREA 700 SQUARE METRES
CONTRACT VALUE £450,000
PHOTOGRAPHER ANNE WORTHINGTON

THE BRINDLEY ARTS CENTRE
.RUNCORN .JOHN MILLER + PARTNERS

On the way to view this new arts centre, the judges studied the images submitted by the architects and debated whether the banded brickwork and curtain-wall-clad stair towers were not a little unfashionable. But arriving at the building, their reservations diminished, and as they entered the curved two-storey foyer the clarity of organization and welcoming environment quickly became clear. This successful orientation space is at the heart of the building. Filled with light, it leads the eye to all of the main events – auditorium, black box, café, bar – and generates a surprising sense of spaciousness that is clearly enjoyed by client and users alike.

There is an assured quality and character in each of the functions. The main auditorium, with its plush purple chairs, exploits its curved composition, generating a large space but one that is intimate enough for small performances. The first-floor studio is distinctive in black and red, and the exhibition space is memorable through its poised picture window.

Externally, the building's position is a good response to its immediate environment, using the canalside to generate views and to provide a generous café terrace. It sits well in its context, and the landscape has been carefully considered.

Finishes are tough and basic but skilful attention to detail has been applied throughout, with a commitment to sustainability and low running costs (the client intends to fit solar control blinds to the café and foyer, omitted from the original contract). Much of the architecture is familiar, but this is a well-mannered building with a strong sense of place that adds much to the civic and local identity of Runcorn in addition to providing plenty of well-planned performance space. A great deal has been achieved with the available budget.

CLIENT HALTON BOROUGH COUNCIL
STRUCTURAL ENGINEER DEWHURST, MACFARLANE & PARTNERS
M&E ENGINEER SVM PARTNERSHIP
THEATRE CONSULTANTS CARR & ANGIER
ACOUSTIC ENGINEERS ARUP ACOUSTICS
CONTRACTOR G. & J. SEDDON LTD
GROSS INTERNAL AREA 2900 SQUARE METRES
CONTRACT VALUE £7.2 MILLION
PHOTOGRAPHER DENNIS GILBERT – VIEW

THE JERWOOD CENTRE .GRASMERE .BENSON + FORSYTH/NAPPER ARCHITECTS

The Jerwood Centre was built to house the Wordsworth Trust's collection of books, manuscripts and fine art, an outstanding archive of national importance. In its context it is a quiet but dramatic building with a wonderful tactile quality mainly achieved through the use of traditional slate and random rubble walling, complementing the elegant contemporary forms of the composition.

The site, in the Town End Conservation Area, is an extremely sensitive one, with adjacent and adjoining listed buildings; planning approval was only achieved by Benson + Forsyth after an appeal in May 1994. Napper Architects have developed the original design and taken it to completion.

The building's organization is both simple and elegant. It comprises two elements: a large rectangular form that houses the main reading-room, storage and archive, and a smaller circular element that houses the poetry reading-room. Joined only at first floor with a finely detailed link, their relationship successfully forms the entry, an interesting route around the building and views to its historic neighbours beyond. Internally, the layout is simple and clear. A large roof, separated by a continuous clerestorey, hovers over the reading-room, while circulation routes are punctuated with windows that provide dramatic views.

This is a beautifully crafted building that emphasizes the contribution that modern architecture can make in even the most sensitive locations. It is a credit to both firms of architects and to the client, who persevered through a difficult planning process to achieve a sensitive contemporary solution when it would have been easier to resort to pastiche.

CLIENT THE WORDSWORTH TRUST
ENGINEER ARUP NEWCASTLE
CONTRACTOR KIER NORTHERN
GROSS INTERNAL AREA 550 SQUARE METRES
CONTRACT VALUE £2.35 MILLION
PHOTOGRAPHER ALEX BLACK

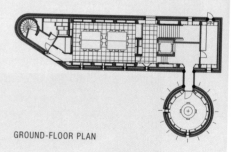

GROUND-FLOOR PLAN

OAK FARM 1
.LIVERPOOL .SHED KM

The building's essential diagram is extremely clear, and this rigour is carried through into the internal organization, choice of materials and detailing. A carefully balanced and harmonious relationship has been achieved between old and new, with the two masonry elements both linked and separated by the glazed entrance hall. The use of the same stone for the extension creates continuity with the original farmhouse, while its minimal detailing ensures there is no competition between the elements.

The spatial arrangement of the interior is simple and effective. There is an economy of expression throughout, and the double-height void of the entrance hall is all the more dramatic for being the only use of this device. Through the careful placement of elements, circulation is subtle and understated.

The building is permeated with thoughtful and intriguing details that are meticulously designed and beautifully executed, using a limited palette of high-quality materials. Although this is in many respects a minimalist design, the choice of materials, in particular the warm Burmese teak (apparently from a sustainable source), generates a homely atmosphere not often found in comparable buildings.

Placing the house along the north edge of the plot, a strategy dictated by the location of the existing farmhouse, has allowed it to be totally open to the south, exploiting impressive views of the garden. The significant expanse of glass encourages the landscape to flow into the interior, and the lowering of the floor relative to the external deck creates a potent and unusual perspective. The orientation of the house also provides natural privacy from neighbours.

This project has an uncomplicated ease. It is Modernist in the best sense of being simple and rational, with attractive proportions, careful attention to detail and an assured integration with its site and the new landscaped elements.

CLIENT JONATHAN FALKINGHAM
STRUCTURAL ENGINEER SUTCLIFFE
CONTRACTORS OAK FARM PARTNERSHIP/ URBAN SPLASH LTD
GROSS INTERNAL AREA 400 SQUARE METRES
CONTRACT VALUE £1 MILLION
PHOTOGRAPHER SHED KM

SHORTLISTED FOR THE MANSER MEDAL

GROUND-FLOOR PLAN

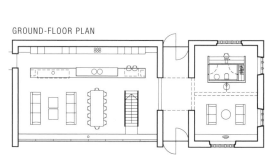

THE PERFORMANCE ACADEMY
.NEWCASTLE UPON TYNE .RMJM LTD

This building represents an interesting resolution to a complicated brief. Its success is largely attributable to the academy director's knowledge and drive, seeking out cost-effective and innovative technical and organizational arrangements for the teaching spaces. However, the architects' contribution is evident in their imaginative responses and the production of a successful piece of architecture within a very tight budget and short timescale.

Fresh and with a strong identity, the scheme does not resort to attention-seeking forms. The use of colour and light with simple, industrial materials – coloured profiled-metal sheet, polycarbonate, steel and concrete – creates the sense of a considered, well-proportioned and efficient building. It sits well in its setting on the edge of the campus and forms an interesting, quiet landmark in the city, visible from the south side of the Tyne.

The jurors liked the way that the 'light' and 'black box' spaces are articulated. The scheme mirrors the front-of-house analogy of a theatre, the foyer-type space providing a lively democratic and social area for the academy and doubling up as breakout space and for special events.

The detailing of the building in terms of the expression of materials and their junctions is generally very good. An exemplary project has produced a piece of good-quality architecture.

CLIENT NEWCASTLE COLLEGE
STRUCTURAL AND BUILDING SERVICES ENGINEER RMJM
PROJECT AND COST MANAGEMENT TURNER AND TOWNSEND
ACOUSTIC AND PERFORMANCE CONSULTANT SANDY BROWN ASSOCIATES
CONTRACTOR SIR ROBERT MCALPINE
GROSS INTERNAL AREA 10,000 SQUARE METRES
CONTRACT VALUE £21 MILLION
PHOTOGRAPHER CHRIS GASCOIGNE

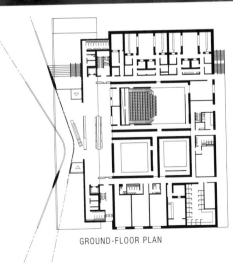

GROUND-FLOOR PLAN

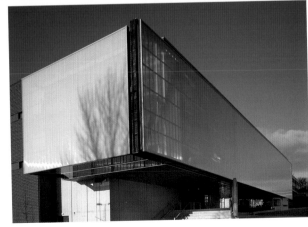

CLASSROOM OF THE FUTURE, MOSSBROOK SCHOOL
.SHEFFIELD .SARAH WIGGLESWORTH ARCHITECTS

The school is for children with special needs, most of whom are autistic, and has the benefit of experienced teaching staff. The architects selected for this project showed a fresh and innovative approach, using appropriate technology ingeniously. There has evidently been a fruitful dialogue between the two sets of professionals in which both parties generated ideas and were prepared to listen and respond.

The building was designed around the needs of the children but it is nevertheless adaptable. It deploys an interesting range of robust materials in an imaginative way, such as ply structure and natural wood-faced linings, combined with high-quality fixtures and some brightly coloured elements. As an ensemble these create a positive and pleasant atmosphere, not just in terms of physical proportions and appearance but also in terms of light, sound, smell and touch. Despite its proximity to a major dual carriageway, the setting of this building is unusually idyllic, with views to open land. The classroom overlooks a pond surrounded by trees, so a feeling of connection with nature prevails.

The architects have included a series of interactive elements, such as webcams set up on the nature reserve that relay pictures to plasma screens in the classrooms; a *camera obscura* also brings the natural world into the classroom. They have incorporated a sound installation devised with the involvement of an artist, and – still more imaginatively – they have left exposed elements of the building's construction; while exhibiting scientific phenomena, it is as engaging for adults as it is for children.

One of the most interesting aspects of this project is the question of whether it can be considered a generic solution that could be rolled out elsewhere or whether its success as a tranquil environment is achieved by virtue of its pleasing contrast to the other classrooms. This is an ongoing debate, but the project claims a strong case for the bottom-up approach to effecting change in schools.

CLIENT SHEFFIELD EDUCATION DIRECTORATE
EXECUTIVE ARCHITECT AND PROJECT MANAGER SHEFFIELD DESIGN AND PROPERTY
STRUCTURAL AND M&E ENGINEER SHEFFIELD DESIGN AND PROPERTY
CONTRACTOR KIER SHEFFIELD
GROSS INTERNAL AREA 142 SQUARE METRES
CONTRACT VALUE £350,000
PHOTOGRAPHERS PETER LATHEY/SUE BARR

SHORTLISTED FOR THE RIBA INCLUSIVE DESIGN AWARD AND THE STEPHEN LAWRENCE PRIZE

SHEFFIELD CITY COUNCIL AND DFES SHORTLISTED FOR CLIENT OF THE YEAR

01 .YORKSHIRE

LONGLEY PARK SIXTH FORM COLLEGE
.SHEFFIELD .ELLIS WILLIAMS ARCHITECTS

This project, in a disadvantaged area of Sheffield, comes over much better in reality than it does in photographs. It is characterized externally by its use of a reddish lignum panel and dark bricks that appear austere but nevertheless have a warmth to them. As quite a large college (taking approximately one thousand students) on a tight site, it is laid out over several storeys and is relatively compact in its planning. However, there is an intriguing progression from the lofty and well-daylit central foyer, via stairs rising up in the space to the upper levels. These become more open and interesting in terms of the corridor/breakout areas towards the top of the building.

The building provides an interesting range of spaces within its apparently uniform set of volumes, generating such a pleasant and dynamic atmosphere for learning that many of the students delay going home after school is over.

Detailing was generally good, robust where necessary, and derived from a controlled and restrained palette of materials. The architects have made use of passive environmental systems, including TermoDeck, and the building is believed to be energy efficient.

This completely new college is a good example of how design can have positive effects on the well-being of an institution and its neighbourhood.

CLIENT LONGLEY PARK SIXTH FORM COLLEGE
STRUCTURAL AND SERVICES ENGINEER BURO HAPPOLD
PROJECT MANAGER AA PROJECTS
PUBLIC ART ART AND ARCHITECTURE
LANDSCAPE PLINKE
CONTRACTOR KIER NORTHERN
GROSS INTERNAL AREA 8370 SQUARE METRES
CONTRACT VALUE £8.5 MILLION
PHOTOGRAPHER PAUL RATTIGAN

SHEFFIELD CITY COUNCIL SHORTLISTED FOR CLIENT OF THE YEAR

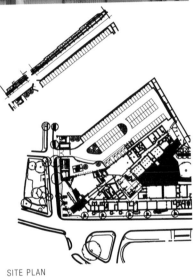

SITE PLAN

CREATIVE ENTERPRISE CENTRE .CAERNARFON .RICHARD MURPHY ARCHITECTS

The Creative Enterprise Centre is a fascinating building, a quayside regeneration project delivered under a design-and-build contract, that uses a combination of arts-based commercial enterprises to give vitality to the building by day, and a multipurpose hall and studios to bring activities to the building by night – the aim being to find new synergies in the overlaps.

The diagram of the building, inspired by its dockside position, is expressed as three parallel warehouse-type structures with corridors between. The higher barn-like central volume accommodates the main performance spaces, rehearsal rooms and a large atrium-foyer. Theatre audiences promenade along the galleries, animating the space; the offices also give on to walkways around the atrium, so that their users' activities are integrated with those of theatregoers.

The principal volume is flanked on each side by a slightly lower and much narrower three-storey office wing. At the north end the three structures create a very clear and highly emotive composition reminiscent of fishermen's net lofts at Hastings. At the south end, however, external secondary escape decks and spiral staircases create an ambiguity about the form: is it three tall and taut timber sheds, or a single more complex structure – a horizontally layered steel-framed cage for multipurpose, and changeable, use? This confusion only adds to the building's great charm. It creates an informality that is extraordinarily seductive.

The building exudes quality. The auditorium, which seats four hundred people on three levels and has variable acoustics to suit speech and music, is particularly superb. It is connected to the outside world in a way theatre spaces seldom are: there is a window from the entrance porch to give visitors their first glimpse of the interior and, at a higher level, a mirrored view of the Menai Straits and Anglesey above the stage – a true piece of theatre.

CLIENT CWMNI TREF CAERNARFON
STRUCTURAL ENGINEER VERYARDS LTD
SERVICES ENGINEER BURO HAPPOLD
PROJECT MANAGER DOIG HART
CONSULTANTS
ACOUSTIC ENGINEER AND THEATRE CONSULTANT SANDY BROWN ASSOCIATES
PLANNING SUPERVISOR WAKEMANS
CONTRACTOR WATKIN JONES CONSTRUCTION
GROSS INTERNAL AREA 3337 SQUARE METRES
CONTRACT VALUE £4.4 MILLION
PHOTOGRAPHER DANIEL HOPKINSON

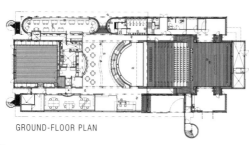

GROUND-FLOOR PLAN

WALES MILLENNIUM CENTRE
.CARDIFF .CAPITA PERCY THOMAS

With devolution adding impetus to the search for a national cultural identity through architecture, the Wales Millennium Centre represents huge ambition. To attempt this under the spotlight of the debate following the demise of Zaha Hadid's design for the Cardiff Bay Opera House would be difficult enough, but to construct such a massive and complex building under a fast-track design-and-build contract is truly Herculean.

Jonathan Adams of Percy Thomas used to work with Will Alsop, and something of his master's voice is apparent in the concern with form. Taking inspiration from the cliffs at Southerndown, Adams developed the concept of strata-like bands formed in a variety of patterns and colours of stone, with a contrasting central volume containing the theatre and fly tower. The surface of the shell is steel plate, with seams and rivets expressing the nature of the material, as the stonework expresses the natural state of the slate.

The main auditorium houses 1900 people in great comfort and with excellent sightlines, while the acoustics have been universally praised. In addition, there is a 250-seat studio theatre, a recording studio, eight rehearsal rooms, and a 100-bed hostel. There are also spaces for many organizations and activities. Add to this the usual back-of-house facilities plus all the foyers, cafés, bars and so on, and this becomes a very testing brief indeed.

The Wales Millennium Centre is the defining feature of the public space that is also addressed by RRP's new Welsh Assembly Building and the old Pier Head Building. Phase 2 – a new building for the National Orchestra of Wales – now has the go-ahead; when finished it will hide the centre's deliberately cheap and cheerful rear elevations. Completion of the Assembly Building will create a new dynamic with its neighbours, and Cardiff will have gained a public space and a suite of buildings in keeping with its capital status.

Although built in difficult circumstances, the Wales Millennium Centre provides good value for money and a beautiful auditorium. Much loved by the Welsh public, it has already gained iconic status.

CLIENT WALES MILLENNIUM CENTRE
STRUCTURAL AND M&E ENGINEER ARUP
ACOUSTIC CONSULTANT ARUP ACOUSTICS
LANDSCAPE ARCHITECT FIRA
PROJECT MANAGER CLARUS CONSULTING
THEATRE CONSULTANT CARR & ANGIER
CONTRACTOR SIR ROBERT MCALPINE
GROSS INTERNAL AREA 35,000 SQUARE METRES
CONTRACT VALUE £78 MILLION
PHOTOGRAPHER SARAH DUNCAN

07 .WALES

SURE START
.TAMWORTH .SJÖLANDER DA CRUZ ARCHITECTS

Sure Start Tamworth is a quirky building right in the frontline of a 1970s estate plagued by vandalism, truancy, drug-use and anti-social behaviour. While its neighbours shelter behind shutters, boards and barbed wire, the Sure Start building is transparent, colourful and cheerful. Its entrance and foyer engage with the surrounding streets and revitalize what was a run-down square in the middle of the estate.

It is an inspiring example of a successful partnership between a determined and intelligent client and an architect who was prepared to devote considerable time and effort to engagement with the community during the design, construction and post-completion phases.

The finished building provides an uplifting and efficient space at the heart of the local community in which to advertise, develop and support all aspects of childcare and parenting skills. It is clearly popular with its users and most of its neighbours, although it is already under assault from gangs of ram-raiding youths and graffiti artists. Nevertheless, it is surviving the onslaught well and is cleverly adapting to these attacks. It provides a hopeful statement for the generations who will grow up in these difficult surroundings, showing that architecture can make a real difference to the lives of people living on a problem estate.

The internal planning is cleverly thought out, with each space performing multiple tasks, and the building clearly operates very effectively. The client was involved to an unusual degree throughout the design and construction process, and this has paid dividends in terms of user satisfaction and in achieving a high-quality finished product.

CLIENT SURE START TAMWORTH
ENGINEER STAFFORDSHIRE COUNTY PROPERTY SERVICES
CONTRACTOR THOMAS VALE
GROSS INTERNAL AREA 400 SQUARE METRES
CONTRACT VALUE £635,000
PHOTOGRAPHER ROD DORLING

SHORTLISTED FOR THE ARCHITECTS' JOURNAL FIRST BUILDING AWARD

GROUND-FLOOR PLAN

78–80 DERNGATE
.NORTHAMPTON .JOHN MCASLAN + PARTNERS

No. 78 Derngate is a narrow-fronted terraced house transformed by Charles Rennie Mackintosh in 1916 and painstakingly restored to its original condition. Next to it, No. 80 is an even narrower terraced house that has been completely rebuilt to function as entrance lobby, circulation space and museum to service its neighbour. Both houses display very little of themselves to the street, and it is a magical experience to walk inside and discover the exuberant late-Mackintosh interiors as well as the calm counterpoint of McAslan's museum-in-a-stairwell. Both share the same attention to detail, making the most of the very restricted space available, and celebrating in radically different ways movement, space, light, colour and texture.

The Mackintosh restoration is an excellent example of creative conservation and reuse. John McAslan + Partners led a multiskilled team of historians, researchers and specialist consultants in producing a work of scholarly conservation. The jury did question whether No. 80, by contrast, could not have been an entirely new building, outside as well as inside, though obviously this would have caused a great deal of controversy. The architects have instead produced a beautifully crafted interior space where the staircase, exhibition cases and intermediate floors are united into one architectural language, very much of the twenty-first century, within an accurately reconstructed version of the eighteenth-century exterior. Attention to detail throughout is exemplary.

The scheme has been a popular and financial success, and the 78 Derngate Trust is now moving on to consider the development of a shop and cafeteria in a property adjacent to No. 80.

CLIENT 78 DERNGATE TRUST
STRUCTURAL ENGINEER JAMPEL, DAVIDSON & BELL
BUILDING SERVICES ENGINEER RYBKA
QS BOYDEN + COMPANY
CONTRACTOR WILLIAM ANELAY LTD
GROSS INTERNAL AREA 325 SQUARE METRES
CONTRACT VALUE £2.5 MILLION
PHOTOGRAPHER RICHARD BRYANT – ARCAID

SHORTLISTED FOR THE CROWN ESTATE CONSERVATION AWARD

GROUND-FLOOR PLAN

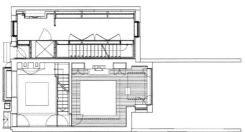

LEICESTER CREATIVE BUSINESS DEPOT
.LEICESTER .ASH SAKULA ARCHITECTS

Of all the projects visited by the East Midlands jury, this one generated most debate and discussion. While there was appreciation of the exuberance of the detailing in both the refurbishment and the new-build elements, there was a general feeling that more impact might have been made with fewer, more robust materials.

In the existing building, the jury liked the lightwell that had been cut into the centre of the building, creating a circulation route around it, and with open and connected spaces off it.

With the new building, the jury enjoyed the attention to detailing of each workspace, with an intriguing arrangement of windows that generated a random theme and a pattern externally, but remained governed by function on the inside. The jury questioned the relationship of structure to exterior cladding, which led to an impression that this too was a conversion rather than a completed twenty-first-century building.

The two buildings enclose a courtyard space with a rather unwelcoming tarmac surface – perhaps a victim of cost-cutting or the design-and-build process – but this might become as well-used and useful a space as the adjacent cafeteria. The artistic interventions on the building, video light work and colourful cladding, were also appreciated.

CLIENT LEICESTER CITY COUNCIL
STRUCTURAL ENGINEER DIAMOND WOOD PARTNERSHIP
PROJECT MANAGEMENT FOCUS CONSULTANTS
CONTRACTOR CLEGG CONSTRUCTION
GROSS INTERNAL AREA 3600 SQUARE METRES
CONTRACT VALUE £4.75 MILLION
PHOTOGRAPHER NICHOLAS KANE

ABODE, NEWHALL
.HARLOW .PROCTOR MATTHEWS

Newhall is a new settlement of 2500 houses being created in two phases on a greenfield site near Harlow and the M11. Although the project is built entirely by the private sector, the government is closely following its development. Here in phase one, Proctor Matthews, which delivered the second part of Ralph Erskine's masterplan for the Greenwich Millennium Village so successfully, has sought to 'develop an architectural vocabulary that combines a contemporary aesthetic and a response to twenty-first-century living patterns with a sensitivity to local materials, colour and texture'.

In fact, the architects have thrown a whole lexicon at the project. Thatch, coloured render, weatherboarding, external stairs, gabions, oriel windows: they are all there, but to some purpose. There is perhaps a lack of architectural editing, but the oriel windows do shade rooms from direct sun; the external staircases obviate the need for fire doors in the three- (or more) storey houses, thus liberating and making more flexible the floor-plans. And the gabions are good for attracting wildlife. The four-storey houses put the living-room at first-floor level, bringing in much-needed light while freeing up the ground floor as workspace, granny flat or teenage retreat. The house can adapt with a family's changing requirements, promoting 'lifetime communities'.

The masterplan lays down a hierarchy of streets, avenues, lanes and mews. Within this hierarchy, a variety of house types adds further interest in a way they seldom do in standard housebuilder estates. Finally, bays, balconies and recesses articulate the streetscape, adding the play of light and shade to façades. This scheme creates characterful neighbourhoods without resorting to Poundbury-style pastiche.

CLIENT COUNTRYSIDE PROPERTIES
MASTERPLANNER ROGER EVANS ASSOCIATES
STRUCTURAL ENGINEER CAMERON TAYLOR BEDFORD
LANDSCAPE DESIGN PIRKKO HIGSON
SERVICES ENGINEER AND CONTRACTOR COUNTRYSIDE PROPERTIES
GROSS INTERNAL AREA 5232 SQUARE METRES
CONTRACT VALUE £10 MILLION
PHOTOGRAPHER TIM CROCKER

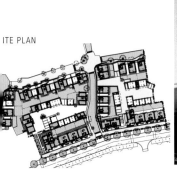

COURTYARD BUILDING, FITZWILLIAM MUSEUM .CAMBRIDGE .JOHN MILLER + PARTNERS

Increasing visitor numbers and growth of its collections and in the needs of conservation, curatorial care and scholarship, education and access for visitors, particularly those with disabilities, had put the Fitzwilliam Museum's existing accommodation under severe pressure. In response, the museum devised a strategy to improve its accommodation and the arrangement of the collections, and to improve access. The courtyard project represents the first major stage of that strategy.

The complex brief for the redevelopment of the southern courtyard involved reconstructing an extension built in the 1970s as well as the new work, which included the provision of public spaces: an entrance hall to provide full accessibility, a new lift, orientation hall, café and shop, a new gallery, renovated existing galleries and stores for reserve collections, and spaces for research, conservation and teaching.

New accommodation is provided both within the envelope of the existing building and in an extension occupying part of an internal courtyard. A continuous rooflight separates the new and the earlier buildings. A double-height winter garden in this space houses the orientation hall, shop and café. Directly linked to this space is an education suite in the extended basement.

This seamless insertion into the Grade I-listed building has been handled with almost clinical precision, belying the considerable technical difficulties of construction. The new building acts as a catalyst, combining and reorganizing new and old spaces with ingenuity and imagination. These spaces operate efficiently and, at the same time, are a pleasure to be in. The architects have successfully designed a facility that both has the capacity to stimulate and engage its occupants and visitors and is excellent in execution and detail.

CLIENT FITZWILLIAM MUSEUM, UNIVERSITY OF CAMBRIDGE
STRUCTURAL ENGINEER CAMPBELL REITH HILL
M&E ENGINEER SVM
PROJECT MANAGER GTMS
CONTRACTOR AMEC
GROSS INTERNAL AREA 5300 SQUARE METRES
CONTRACT VALUE £10 MILLION
PHOTOGRAPHER DENNIS GILBERT – VIEW

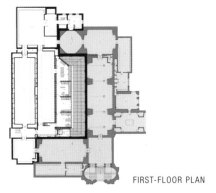

FIRST-FLOOR PLAN

FITZWILLIAM COLLEGE GATEHOUSE AND AUDITORIUM
.CAMBRIDGE .ALLIES AND MORRISON

The Gatehouse Court completes Denys Lasdun's masterplan for Fitzwilliam College, giving it a new frontage and reorientating the college to the south. Lasdun himself designed the first college courts and central building (the library, dining hall, junior common room and bar) and their construction was complete by 1963. The development provides forty en-suite student rooms, two seminar rooms, a bigger porters' lodge, staff offices and IT facilities. As well as accommodating students during term, the rooms generate invaluable conference revenue in the vacations. All the new facilities have proved popular with their users, with the new rooms coming top in the annual ballot for rooms in college – although some students have apparently complained that the shutters prevent them putting their trainers out to air on window ledges; such is Allies and Morrison's legendary attention to detail.

The other element is a new theatre that links to the college gardens. This is a flexible space that is as suited to badminton as it is to music or drama. International performers have praised the acoustic (which is adjustable for music or speech). Retractable seating allows the auditorium to seat anything between 50 and 250 people, making for ever-full houses.

The new buildings have given self-belief to a relatively new and distinctly unstuffy Cambridge college. They are stylish, not least in their subtle use of the college colours of burgundy and silver-grey; and they work. What more could a client ask for?

CLIENT FITZWILLIAM COLLEGE, UNIVERSITY OF CAMBRIDGE
STRUCTURAL AND SERVICES ENGINEER WHITBYBIRD
PLANNING CONSULTANT CARILLION
THEATRE CONSULTANT (CONCEPT) CARR AND ANGIER
LANDSCAPE ARCHITECT CAMBRIDGE LANDSCAPE ARCHITECTS
ACOUSTIC CONSULTANT ARUP ACOUSTICS
CONTRACTOR MARRIOTT CONSTRUCTION
GROSS INTERNAL AREA 2975 SQUARE METRES
CONTRACT VALUE £8.2 MILLION
PHOTOGRAPHER PETER COOK – VIEW

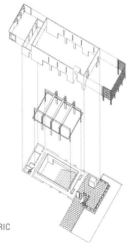

EXPLODED AXONOMETRIC

HEADQUARTERS OF THE CAMBRIDGE FEDERATION OF WOMEN'S INSTITUTES
.CAMBRIDGE .ELLISMILLER

The local authority, for reasons best known to itself, decreed that the proposed Women's Institute headquarters building should be no bigger than the pig-farrowing shed that occupied the site and for which the WI swapped its former Cambridge townhouse HQ – doubtless a pretty canny piece of property dealing. The building provides offices for the secretariat, conference facilities for fifty people, catering and toilets to be used by around forty local groups with a total membership of 4000 women.

On a low budget, the architects have achieved a building that delights and functions well. It is ingenious, and almost every detail has been considered lovingly. In keeping with the WI's commitment to Local Agenda 21, the principles of sustainability have informed the project throughout. From the choice of location (on a major bus route to encourage people to use public transport); the choice of materials (the building incorporates recycling of the original structure and that of a number of smaller buildings on the site); to the incorporation of active measures, such as external shutters to control solar gain, photovoltaics to generate electricity and a rain-water harvesting and storage system; all of these factors combine to produce a building that is well-tempered and comfortable to use.

Much-loved by its users, this is an exemplary piece of work, where the extent of innovation is matched by the rigour and integrity of the detailing. Every student should visit it to learn how more may be achieved with less.

CLIENT CAMBRIDGE FEDERATION OF WOMEN'S INSTITUTES
STRUCTURAL ENGINEER WHITBYBIRD
SERVICES ENGINEER ROGER PARKER ASSOCIATES
QS HENRY RILEY
CONTRACTOR BRITANNIABUILD LTD
GROSS INTERNAL AREA 170 SQUARE METRES
CONTRACT VALUE £307,000
PHOTOGRAPHER TIMOTHY SOAR

SHORTLISTED FOR THE RIBA SUSTAINABILITY AWARD

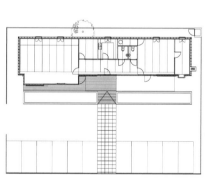

FLOOR PLAN

NORWICH CATHEDRAL REFECTORY .NORWICH .HOPKINS ARCHITECTS

The scheme emerged from a design competition to provide visitor facilities adjacent to a Grade I-listed building. Proposals by other architects were more timid: remote, isolated structures that neither threatened the existing historic structure nor engaged with it. Hopkins's brave scheme succeeds in resolving the whole precinct of buildings in what is one of the most beautiful of all English cathedral closes.

The scheme is just phase one of a three-stage Norwich Cathedral Visitors' Centre project. This building houses a restaurant, toilets, administrative offices and a new entrance to the medieval cathedral library. As well as bringing the cathedral, so far as is possible, in line with the Disability Discrimination Act, the new work restores the original cloisters as the main circulation route around the building.

Working with a relatively modest budget, the architects have created a building that is brilliant in concept and execution. A beautiful two-storey timber and glass building has been carefully abutted to the existing cloisters and directly around the fragments of the old refectory building, largely demolished at the time of the Reformation. Rooflights along one edge bring in daylight through leaded windows. The roof oversails the main timber structure, leaving triple-height spaces at either glazed end. These not only bring in additional light, they also accommodate the main means of circulation: entrances, stairs and lift.

From ground level, stairs guide the visitor up to the refreshment facilities. The use of materials and the quality of detailing gives the first-floor refectory an air of tranquillity and contemplation (the service facilities, such as the WCs and staff accommodation, are located discreetly below). This design has a timeless quality and the capacity to endure as a fine work of architecture throughout its working life.

CLIENT THE DEAN AND CHAPTER OF NORWICH CATHEDRAL
STRUCTURAL AND SERVICES ENGINEER BURO HAPPOLD
CONTRACTOR R.G. CARTER, NORWICH
GROSS INTERNAL AREA 987 SQUARE METRES
CONTRACT VALUE £3.2 MILLION
PHOTOGRAPHERS PAUL TYAGI/RICHARD DAVIES

LEVEL 0 PLAN

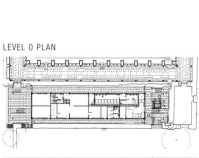

NAUTILUS APARTMENTS
.WESTWARD HO! .GUY GREENFIELD ARCHITECTS

As in so many faded English seaside towns, in Westward Ho! demand for traditional holidays has declined. In its place this project offers a new type of property. Made up of twenty-eight units, Nautilus Apartments is a high-density seafront development that stands out from its neighbours and takes on the challenge of embodying the power and movement of the ocean. This ambition is successfully carried through with an extraordinary degree of control from planning to detailing.

The plan, a section of an Archimedean spiral (a nautilus shell), is arranged in fourteen units, each with three floors of accommodation. Each unit has glazed ends with views out to sea. As the plan spirals, each unit gradually increases in width, while in section each is very slightly lower. Offset from one another, the resulting effect within each apartment combines privacy with proximity to the expanse of water ahead. Likewise, the top-floor apartments are energized by a slot of sky that runs from front to back, created where frameless glazing separates the masonry walls from the floating roof above.

Guy Greenfield, shortlisted for the 2001 Stirling Prize with his innovative doctors' surgery in Hammersmith, London, has here become his own client. Using direct labour, the project presents a refreshing model that defines new ways of working and questions the role an architect can assume. Equally, it demonstrates the role contemporary architecture can take as a catalyst for urban regeneration. This is strong architecture, setting itself against the forces of nature; but at the same time it is light, ethereal, momentary and timeless.

While the seaside is a place of frivolity, there is an undercurrent present; a respect for nature and the dynamic force that may suddenly be unleashed. This project is brave, confident and inspiring. It sums up the contradictions and contrasts of its location, and sets a new standard for architecture beside the sea.

CLIENT AND MAIN CONTRACTOR GUY GREENFIELD ARCHITECTS
STRUCTURAL ENGINEER COOPER ASSOCIATES
GROSS INTERNAL AREA 2520 SQUARE METRES
CONTRACT VALUE £2.5 MILLION
PHOTOGRAPHER PAUL TYAGI

THE CAMPUS .WESTON-SUPER-MARE .DAVID MORLEY ARCHITECTS

Award-winning architecture can exist in the least likely location. Here, on the edge of Weston-Super-Mare, between numerous housing developments and a retail park, a truly enlightened client set out to re-evaluate what makes a community building, what makes a school, and to see whether, by combining local facilities under one roof, a new type of building could be achieved.

The Campus combines a range of activities: a library, council one-stop shop, meeting rooms, college facilities, a primary school and nursery, along with a school for children with severe learning disabilities. Also included are sports and changing facilities, both indoor and out, a skateboard park and a hydrotherapy pool. To make this as a sustainable building on a modest budget is no mean achievement.

Given the budget, brief and timetable, and with the added challenge of creating an accessible and inclusive environment, this scheme is truly inspiring. It positively sings with thought and care, even in the face of value engineering and a very tight programme. It has surpassed its objectives, even when it has had to negotiate boundaries between competing and contradictory functions. It is undoubtedly innovative, and an exemplar of a building type: the community hub. To make this all happen it needed an exceptional client. Here, Russ Currie was single-minded and persistent in building consensus.

The building had to be flexible and permeable. As a result, it almost breathes as it changes shape to accommodate the complex timetable. Boundaries dissolve and fluctuate over the day; a school hall can cater for lunch and later that day accommodate an exercise class. A reception desk can be a library checkout point while also serving coffee and letting people pay bills. To use a term invented by Rem Koolhaas, this is cross programming, where combining functions in new and unexpected combinations creates hybrid spaces that take on a force of their own. It is a socially derived architecture designed to accommodate the unplanned and the evolving.

CLIENT NORTH SOMERSET COUNCIL
PROJECT MANAGER AND QS DICKSON POWELL PARTNERSHIP
STRUCTURAL ENGINEER PRICE & MYERS
M&E ENGINEER MAX FORDHAM LLP
LANDSCAPE ARCHITECT LIVINGSTON EYRE ASSOCIATES
PLANNING SUPERVISOR GARDINER & THEOBALD PLANNING SUPERVISION
CONTRACTOR KIER WESTERN
GROSS INTERNAL AREA 5389 SQUARE METRES
CONTRACT VALUE £9 MILLION
PHOTOGRAPHER MORLEY VON STERNBERG

PRIVATE HOUSE
.GLOUCESTER .JAMIESON ASSOCIATES ARCHITECTS

The farmhouse is Grade II-listed and has absorbed changes and layers of occupation from the seventeenth century onwards. Today, its latest evolution sees the careful removal of unsympathetic extensions to the main house and a new connection to what had been a cart-shed. This is achieved by the insertion of a modem glass structure, practically a 6-metre cube, that bridges the gap between the two original buildings.

The existing house is also extended in two places by random rubblestone lean-to structures, each topped with a catslide stone roof. Within the scope of the project these vernacular elements sit comfortably without any attempt to conceal their origins; fine slots of glass mark the junction between the new and old elements so that legibility and a sense of layered history are maintained.

This project stands out as an exemplary illustration of contemporary architecture within an historic context. The members of the jury were spellbound as they experienced the sequence of spaces. The architects have not obviously altered the quality of the original main rooms within the house; instead, innovation is concentrated in the circulation spaces. As a result, the connecting spaces are drenched in natural light, while the original rooms manage to maintain an appropriate sense of interior comfort. The spaces designed for movement become places of significance and delight and allow the surrounding landscape to enter the building. At a detailed level, the design of the handrail – a sinuous bronze ribbon floating on slim glass balustrades above stone stairs in the glass cube – manifests respect for both the original and the newly constructed.

Despite a very generous budget and its status as a luxurious country retreat, the project maintains a sense of modesty and timeless calm.

CLIENT PRIVATE
STRUCTURAL ENGINEER MARK LOVELL DESIGN ENGINEERS
SERVICES ENGINEER SHARPE & HOWSE
CONTRACTOR CRANATT CONSTRUCTION LTD
CONTRACT VALUE £450,000
PHOTOGRAPHER NICK MEERS

ALTON LIBRARY
.ALTON .HAMPSHIRE COUNTY COUNCIL ARCHITECTS

Alton's new public library is located on a corner site in the heart of the traditional Hampshire town, next door to the old library, a redundant civil-defence building that will be redeveloped to part-finance this project.

The site is an irregular shape. However, the clever inclusion of the retaining wall (a party wall) to the north has yielded valuable and interesting internal floor area at ground level, and serves to anchor the building firmly to its site. The formal rectangular volume of the upper floors sits above this.

The public approaches the library from an open paved area at the corner of Vicarage Hill and enters the building at one end. The building is arranged on three floors. The main lending stock and the children's library are at ground level, while the first floor is dedicated to quieter, reference use. On the third floor staff restrooms and workrooms, together with publicly accessible meeting rooms, are housed beneath the pitched roof, with top light from integrated rooflights – a very pleasant working environment. The building organization is clearly legible and security is well managed.

Staircases (doubling as means of escape) at each end of the plan provide access to the upper floors. Careful attention has been paid to their design. The judges particularly enjoyed the quiet nature of these spaces, and the incorporation of contemporary timber dados lent a quality to the public circulation spaces.

The design of the building aims to make it clear that it is open to the public. The reading areas have big windows providing views of the town, and solar protection is provided by large timber louvres that give scale and texture. The careful choice of chromatically similar brick and roof tiles, and the bold detailing of the gutters and downpipes, have resulted in a building that is in harmony with its setting and the buildings around it, while having a strong contemporary architectural quality.

CLIENT HAMPSHIRE COUNTY COUNCIL
STRUCTURAL ENGINEER R.J. WATKINSON ASSOCIATES
MECHANICAL ENGINEER HAMPSHIRE COUNTY COUNCIL
QS GRANT ASSOCIATES
CONTRACTOR RICHARDSONS (NYEWOOD) LTD
GROSS INTERNAL AREA 740 SQUARE METRES
CONTRACT VALUE £1.27 MILLION
PHOTOGRAPHER PETER COOK – VIEW

HAMPSHIRE COUNTY COUNCIL SHORTLISTED FOR CLIENT OF THE YEAR

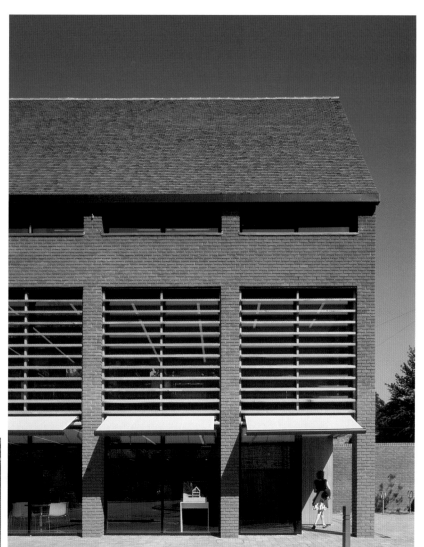

CHEMISTRY RESEARCH LABORATORY, UNIVERSITY OF OXFORD
.OXFORD .RMJM LTD

This new laboratory provides facilities for five hundred postgraduate students and staff, aiming to unite and to mix three separate groups of researchers. The six-storey building comprises three main elements: the laboratory block and the offices, separated by an atrium that houses the restaurant and key social space for the occupants. This is a very impressive and popular space and is no doubt a major draw for attracting new business.

The upper floors of the lab building required flexible generic laboratory space with immediately adjacent writing-up areas; great attention has been paid to the detailed design of these modular units. Circulation of people, handling of chemicals and co-ordination of services (there are around four hundred fume cupboards) are particularly well and efficiently dealt with.

The exemplary planning of the building has resulted in an efficient yet spirited and united faculty. Perhaps the most striking innovation is the controlled presence of daylight and views of other people into and from the modular laboratories, resulting in a light, bright and enjoyable place to work – never easy to achieve in the inevitably internalized environment of the laboratory – and a factor that is aiding the dissemination of knowledge, as the client had hoped.

CLIENT UNIVERSITY OF OXFORD
STRUCTURAL AND BUILDING SERVICES ENGINEER FABER MAUNSELL
QS TURNER & TOWNSEND
CLADDING CONSULTANT ARUP FAÇADE ENGINEERING
FIRE ENGINEERING JEREMY GARDNER ASSOCIATES
PLANNING SUPERVISOR NORTHCROFT
CONTRACTOR LAING O'ROURKE MIDLANDS
GROSS INTERNAL AREA 15,750 SQUARE METRES
CONTRACT VALUE £47.8 MILLION
PHOTOGRAPHER CHRIS GASCOIGNE

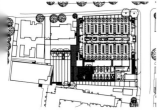

GROUND-FLOOR PLAN

THE GRANARY, CROWMARSH BATTLE FARM
.PRESTON CROWMARSH .SPRATLEY & WOODFIELD

Crowmarsh Battle Farm is a working arable farm. A move to diversify into rural commercial sectors has involved the refurbishment of a number of redundant agricultural buildings for office and other uses. Immediately adjacent to the listed farmhouse, a derelict Grade II timber granary dating from around 1800 has been repaired and converted as a private office for the farm owner, the client for this project, who now runs the business from this building.

The structure was in a very poor state of repair, with significant subsidence beneath the fourteen saddlestones on which it stands, the result of lack of rain-water drainage since the building was constructed. The timbers in the frame were in very poor condition, rotting and insect-infested. To make work to the foundations and below-ground services possible, the entire structure was craned to an area nearby where the timber frame was repaired, retaining most of the original elements. The building was then lifted back to its original site, where the alteration work was undertaken.

The building has been thermally insulated to a high standard beneath the timber wall linings, giving it a new lease of life. Workmanship appears to be of a very high order. Toilet facilities are provided in the form of a contemporary pod, and a new stair has been inserted. New elements are clearly expressed and neatly detailed in a contemporary manner, clearly distinguishing new from old. Where grain-bin partitions have been removed, the archaeology of their positions remains as tenon holes in the floors.

This is an exemplary essay in how to repair and exploit the character of an historic structure while upgrading its physical performance to sustain the needs of the next generation of users. Although the project is small in scale, the lessons learned should extend far beyond this Oxfordshire farm, into a countryside where subsidies are a thing of the past, and where set-aside and the reuse of agricultural land and buildings are now the norm.

CLIENT CROWMARSH BATTLE FARMS LTD
STRUCTURAL ENGINEER CLIVE HUDSON ASSOCIATES
QS MCBAINS COOPER
CONTRACTOR E.W. BEARD LTD
GROSS INTERNAL AREA 86 SQUARE METRES
CONTRACT VALUE £114,000
PHOTOGRAPHER SUSIE BARKER

SHORTLISTED FOR THE CROWN ESTATE CONSERVATION AWARD

GROUND-FLOOR PLAN

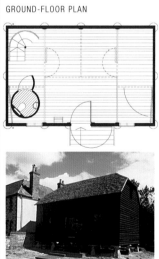

WESTON ADVENTURE PLAYGROUND
.SOUTHAMPTON .FINCH MACINTOSH ARCHITECTS

The site is on the fringe of historic woodland at the foot of Canberra Towers, twenty-three storeys of uncompromising local-authority housing. Levels across the site are difficult, with a 6-metre fall and some gradients of 1:3. The project involved remodelling external play areas and constructing a new indoor play facility and covered space for pre-school to eighteen-year-old local children and their parents. All areas, both internal and external, are fully accessible.

The funders expected a single-storey concrete-block building to replace their dilapidated shed – a solution they felt most appropriate for such a tough neighbourhood. However, the designers persuaded them that another option existed. The result – a timber fort on top of a stockade – resorts to neither stereotype nor pastiche.

The playground is entered through the fortress wall directly beneath the playroom structure, which is supported on steel columns. Valuable covered external play space has thus been liberated and this has become the threshold between the housing estate and the world of children's play. Within the playroom, a large, flexible, daylit space with copious storage is provided. A slightly elevated gallery runs the length of the building at tree-top level and gives a great vantage point over the woodland and the water beyond. The use of wood, galvanized steel and repaintable render on the building and in the play areas gives a consistent, robust quality to the centre.

Local people particularly value the quality of design and materials, which, to their minds, is normally reserved for the rich. Although abundant on the surrounding estate, there is no graffiti in or around the playground.

This project gets every last square inch of use out of a difficult site, and it is possible for a child in a wheelchair to enjoy all aspects of the playground. It is simple but well-executed, robust, usable and clearly loved by staff, children and the wider community. Delivering all this on an extremely tight budget reflects a successful collaboration between client and designers.

CLIENT WESTON ADVENTURE PLAYGROUND
LANDSCAPING SCANDOR LANDSCAPE CONTRACTORS LTD
STRUCTURAL ENGINEER R.J. WATKINSON ASSOCIATES
PLAYGROUND EQUIPMENT PLAYGROUND SERVICES LTD
QS SELWAY JOYCE
CONTRACTOR JOHN HOBDEN LTD
GROSS INTERNAL AREA 297 SQUARE METRES
CONTRACT VALUE £679,762
PHOTOGRAPHER JOE LOW

SHORTLISTED FOR THE RIBA INCLUSIVE DESIGN AWARD AND FOR THE RIBA SUSTAINABILITY AWARD

IGHTHAM MOTE
.SEVENOAKS .STUART PAGE ARCHITECTS

Originally built in 1320, this unique moated house has a complex architectural history and over the centuries has seen major changes to accommodate fashion or to provide more space and comfort. This work in the south-west quarter of Ightham Mote completes a multiphase, £10 million project, the National Trust's largest conservation project of the kind since 1989. Its scope is massive; photographic records show evidence of major structural reconstruction and layer upon layer of different finishes repaired and conserved. One of the most delicate aspects of the work involved the removal of temporary steel trusses, put in to support the roof when the property was acquired by the Trust in 1985, but now threatening to cause its collapse. The timber frame, which proved to be original, has been repaired and made safe.

The south elevation is much photographed but more Victorian than medieval. Instead of rendering over unsound timber studding dating from 1900, it was decided to adopt a more radical approach and reinstate the original frame in English oak with traditional draw-pegged joints.

Internally, most of the rooms were panelled; removal of the panelling for restoration revealed a mix of wallpaper, paint and earlier panelling underneath. Each of these was recorded, conserved and the outer panelling reinstated, thus preserving the complex history of the house.

Project archaeologist Peter Leach worked closely with the architects and contractors from the outset, recording and analysing the structure and its history in order to inform decisions about repair and conservation. The quality of the work undertaken is without doubt first class.

CLIENT THE NATIONAL TRUST
STRUCTURAL ENGINEER MICHAEL BOYLES
ARCHAEOLOGIST PETER LEACH
QS D.R. NOLANS & CO.
CONTRACTOR R.J. BARWICK & SON LTD
GROSS INTERNAL AREA 505 SQUARE METRES
CONTRACT VALUE £1.8 MILLION
PHOTOGRAPHER STUART PAGE ARCHITECTS

SHORTLISTED FOR THE CROWN ESTATE CONSERVATION AWARD

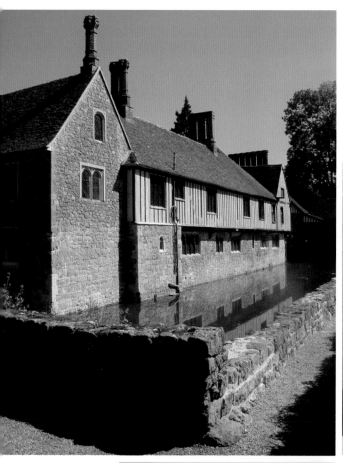

PRIVATE HOUSE
.ASHURSTWOOD .DAVID REA ARCHITECTS

The project is based on what were originally two tiny farm cottages that were somewhat unsatisfactorily knocked into one some years ago. The brief was therefore to create a larger living space with views over the garden. This space would be sunlit by day, but warm and protected at night. The response changes the orientation of the building by moving the main entrance to the west, using it as a device to define a generous new entrance space. The modern intervention creates a shield to provide greater privacy to the garden. The new building includes an artist's studio and a main living space, with framed views into the landscaped garden.

Both from a work and a social point of view, the design has been tailored to the artist's needs, and the client is genuinely happy with the result. The new building has character and charm. Small and intimate, the series of interlocking volumes feels appropriate to the site and garden, and as a foil to the existing rooms in the cottage. On entry, the interior spaces immediately feel right, with good natural lighting. The internal and external composition works exceptionally well, with a good use of materials; the knot-free larch and lead cladding are particularly successful.

The views out of the building are beautifully orchestrated, and at night internally folding translucent screens can be opened out to secure the property. For a first building, this is a very bold and confident scheme.

CLIENT PRIVATE
ENGINEER IAN RUSSELL
CONTRACTOR VALLEY BUILDERS LTD
GROSS INTERNAL AREA 98 SQUARE METRES
CONTRACT VALUE £126,000
PHOTOGRAPHER DAVID REA ARCHITECTS

PRIVATE HOUSE
.HOVE .BBM SUSTAINABLE DESIGN LTD
WITH MILK DESIGN

This house, a remodelled 1950s villa, has been radically extended: out, to create a new studio; up, to provide an extra floor of bedrooms; and back, to make a new living-room with a large balcony. So it is a house within a house, in the manner of Eldridge Smerin's reworking of a Manasseh house in Hampstead for John and Frances Sorrell, shortlisted for the Stirling Prize in 2001. The client, an interior designer, artist and furniture designer who collaborated closely with the architects throughout, is extremely happy with the completed project. An ambitious scheme, it should be acknowledged as a creative and welcome modern intervention in relatively conservative Hove.

The strong visual form of the house provides a powerful and positive contrast to its neighbours. The asymmetrical pitched roof also adds a different dynamic to the streetscape.

Stimulating and engaging, the scheme has internal clarity, and movement through the house is enjoyable and uplifting. There is good use of natural materials, and the detailing is beautifully done. The simple but integrated landscape scheme, designed with the client, connects internal and external spaces effortlessly.

The design has a strong environmental agenda, using jute and recycled-newspaper insulation, clay plasters, organic paints, locally produced sweet chestnut cladding, underfloor heating (with a gas-fired combination boiler) and solar panels. Retention of the 1950s building was considered more sustainable than demolition, even though it presented problems – not least in the myriad of different types of walls – but it is now very difficult to discern new from old.

The project proves that green buildings can be successfully delivered in an entirely contemporary idiom, and the architects, clients and, not least, planners are to be commended for it.

CLIENT PRIVATE
CONSULTANT ENGINEER BEP
CONTRACTOR CHALMERS & CO. LTD
GROSS INTERNAL AREA 277 SQUARE METRES
CONTRACT VALUE £250,000
PHOTOGRAPHER LEIGH SIMPSON

SHORTLISTED FOR THE MANSER MEDAL

GROUND-FLOOR PLAN

ST AUGUSTINE'S RC PRIMARY SCHOOL
.HYTHE .CHENEY THORPE & MORRISON

The school, a low-lying structure on an exposed hillside overlooking the sea, is like an architect's pencil line drawn across the landscape. The curved sweeping roof follows the contours of the slope with a large overhang to protect the glazing on the south elevation from direct sunlight. The building sits comfortably in its setting, and the materials and colours blend well. Durable materials have been used, including cedar cladding, render, and beach stones in the gabion wall. The school is the very opposite of the tough urban academies being built in London but addresses its brief and context just as well.

The building immediately feels uplifting and fun. The scale of the external and internal spaces is appropriate, and the children and staff are quick to say how much they like it. The simple plan provides naturally ventilated interlocking spaces, designed from a child's perspective. Each classroom has views towards the sea, an external timber-decked and sun-protected area, as well as a cantilevered external teaching area sitting on a gabion wall. Everything has been considered, including display areas in a spacious continuous corridor linking colour-coded rooms and cloakrooms with low porthole windows. The clearly defined flexible teaching pods are friendly and filled with natural light; even the toilets are fun and well designed.

The building uses daylight exceptionally well, and it has a naturally ventilated high-thermal-mass structure, grey-water and underfloor-heating systems. Security is well thought through, with the reception class positioned furthest from the entrance, with its own secure playground and covered play space.

CLIENT ARCHDIOCESE OF SOUTHWARK
STRUCTURAL ENGINEER GARY GABRIEL ASSOCIATES
M&E ENGINEER STEVEN NIXON ASSOCIATES
LANDSCAPE ARCHITECT LLOYD BORE
QS AND PLANNING SUPERVISOR BANKS WOOD & PARTNERS
CONTRACTOR GSE DESIGN & BUILD LTD
GROSS INTERNAL AREA 1279 SQUARE METRES
CONTRACT VALUE £2.4 MILLION
PHOTOGRAPHER P.R.W. FREEMAN

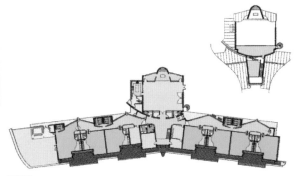

PLANS

VISITOR CENTRE, WAKEHURST PLACE
.ARDINGLY .WALTERS AND COHEN

The Visitor and Interpretation Centre is sited at the entrance to the 200-hectare estate, accommodating visitor information, toilet facilities, ticketing, catering, shop, offices and an external plant nursery. It complements the Millennium Seedbank, Stanton Williams's RIBA Award-winning scheme of 2001, and is part of a growing portfolio of good architecture commissioned by the Royal Botanic Gardens. The new building has also to pay respect to the unique character of Elizabethan Wakehurst Place, owned by the National Trust.

The building is specifically designed to meet the requirements of Part M of the Building Regulations (access to and use of buildings), and describes itself as a sustainable building, which conforms to good practice in energy conservation. The centre attracts large numbers of older visitors, and the design responds sensitively to this factor, catering for all regardless of age, gender or disability.

The centre is sensitively and discreetly located, and appropriate use of materials and colours helps it to sit very comfortably within the landscape. A restrained and elegant steel and glass structure allows the eye to pass through the building and register the beautiful landscape beyond. Louvered timber canopies successfully run the full length of the main elevations, not only shading and breaking up the mass of the building but also activating the architectural composition by the resulting play of light.

The solid timber end stops to the building work well with the internal counters and doorways, detailed as if carved out of the solid. Less successful is the fit-out, particularly in the shop, done at the client's insistence by other hands. However, the flexible nature of the building means that the interior can be improved over time.

CLIENT ROYAL BOTANIC GARDENS, KEW
STRUCTURAL ENGINEER MICHAEL BARCLAY PARTNERSHIP
LANDSCAPE ARCHITECT CHRIS BLANDFORD ASSOCIATES
QS FANSHAWE
SERVICES ENGINEER WATERMAN GORE
CONTRACTOR R. DURTNELL & SONS LTD
GROSS INTERNAL AREA 950 SQUARE METRES
CONTRACT VALUE £1.5 MILLION
PHOTOGRAPHER DENNIS GILBERT – VIEW/ WALTERS AND COHEN

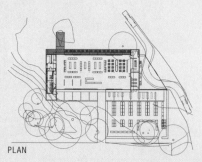

PLAN

ARTISTS' STUDIO
.LONDON NW1 .SANEI HOPKINS ARCHITECTS
WITH HUGHES MEYER STUDIO

For many years the clients, an artist and a potter, have had their garden terminated by a two-storey brick mews factory building with various lean-to additions. After the company that had used the building relocated, the clients acquired it to provide a studio and gallery space coupled with some leisure facilities, the brief requiring space for both 'cerebral and corporeal pleasures'. This building responds successfully to that very particular brief and is well executed.

The proposed design cleared away the lean-to additions, returning the mews building to its original form, and then extended the roof slope on the garden side to create a contrasting volume defined by glass and a mirrored roof plane. The mews building is strongly expressed as a two-storey brick enclosure, the storeys being linked by a glass staircase rising in a void next to the rear façade. This original rear façade, no longer external, has simple brickwork openings unambiguously linking old and new. The full width of the extension uses glass for the sloping and vertical faces, and the horizontal roof, which links them, is completely encased in mirror. The use of mirror is repeated in the cladding of the orthogonal sauna box that interrupts the glazed wall framing the view of the garden. A white-clad steam room, the only other enclosure, rises anthropomorphically from the floor and resonates with the forms in the client's landscape paintings, which are displayed or stacked nearby. The window wall frames the view to the garden.

The use of mirror for all faces of the roof plane and for the sauna box helps to engage the interior and exterior spaces, and the reflections of sky, brickwork, garden and art animate the experience of the building without being overbearing or disorientating. At night the robust simplicity of the mews building is thrown into relief.

CLIENTS PHILIP AND PSICHE HUGHES
STRUCTURAL ENGINEER TECHNIKER LTD
CONTRACTOR CLAREMONT REFURBISHMENT LTD
GROSS INTERNAL AREA 135 SQUARE METRES
CONTRACT VALUE £260,000
PHOTOGRAPHER SUE BARR

SHORTLISTED FOR THE STEPHEN LAWRENCE PRIZE

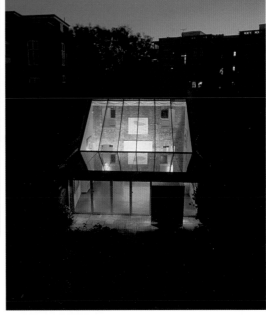

ASPREY
.LONDON W1 .FOSTER AND PARTNERS

The design team had both to provide an updated image for a long-established British luxury-goods company and to address the very particular demands of linking five listed buildings in a coherent and accessible way. The site forms the northern part of a block with three street frontages and, inevitably, floor levels differ from building to building.

The key space that now unites the shop was the backyards of the buildings; by using these previously unplanned spaces to create a glass-roofed courtyard, the individual buildings are appreciated, a focal point created and the circulation routes made legible. This found space is given added definition by the mirror-clad south wall that renders legible the ad hoc relationships of the buildings that define it. The original elements and details of the buildings are thrown into contrast by the confident use of a restrained palette of materials for the new interventions, including a sweeping curved staircase, a *tour de force* rising effortlessly through the space and just touching the adjacent buildings where access is required. The geometry of the glazed roof confidently abuts the existing buildings and reads as a unifying cap to the space.

The façades of the Georgian buildings have been carefully restored, as have features such as cornicing, while the volumes of the interiors have been respected, with detailing of floor finishes and wall linings acknowledging previously removed walls. Mechanical- and electrical-servicing needs have been addressed by using a suspended multipurpose panel in each room. The panel is expressed as a distinct element floating below the ceiling and illuminating the cornicing and adjacent soffit. Throughout, the excellence of the detailing and construction matches the quality of the materials used and provides a tactile as well as a visual delight.

With nine staircases, circulation is considerably easier than one envisages from a floor plan, and the client's need for a coherent whole has been more than satisfied.

CLIENT ASPREY LONDON
STRUCTURAL ENGINEER ALAN BAXTER & ASSOCIATES
M&E ENGINEER TROUP BYWATERS & ANDERS
INTERIOR DESIGNER MLINARIC HENRY AND ZERUDACHI
CONTRACTORS WALLIS (EXTERIOR)/ SIMPSON YORK LTD (INTERIOR)
GROSS INTERNAL AREA 930 SQUARE METRES
CONTRACT VALUE CONFIDENTIAL
PHOTOGRAPHERS DENNIS GILBERT – VIEW/ NIGEL YOUNG

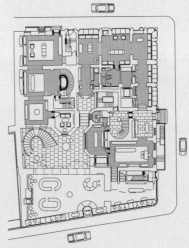

GROUND-FLOOR PLAN

BBC MEDIA VILLAGE, WHITE CITY
.LONDON W12 .ALLIES AND MORRISON

The architects had two tasks: masterplanning the BBC's large White City site to create an identifiable (and secure) 'place' for the organization while allowing for public permeability; and designing two large buildings (and three smaller ones) with inspiring but flexible workspace for some 3800 people. The response was based on a clear strategy with a pair of large functional buildings – the Media and Broadcast Centres – as high as the existing six-storey structure. The new buildings are placed roughly parallel to this to form a cranked open space 30 metres wide. This 'Boulevard', well landscaped with timber benches and event areas, has a generous feel. At ground level there are shops and cafés.

To avoid presenting the rear of the large centres to the road, two office structures of intermediate scale front the street. These have a clearly different materiality and so do not read as part of the BBC. Further pleasantly landscaped spaces (for use by BBC workers only) are sited between the offices and the Media and Broadcast Centres. The Energy Centre completes the northern end of the ensemble, forming a buffer to the A40.

The buildings themselves are robust. Their plans offer spatial flexibility, using slim atriums to structure bands of 18-metre-deep work areas. Open and airy, they have largely been taken over by the teams and departments that inhabit them. Informal meeting and social areas were deliberately planned to encourage such adoption, but the workspaces themselves allow personalization within the buildings' geometric and material discipline.

Concrete, a tactile reddish timber, glass and aluminium dominate; against this background many small meeting rooms facing the atriums have been clad by the users, creating identities within the whole. A further range of colours has been selected by artist Yuko Shiraishi and applied by the architects to the interior. The resulting visual variety means that the relatively corporate exteriors of the buildings belie the stimulating work environments inside.

CLIENTS BBC IN PARTNERSHIP WITH LAND SECURITIES
STRUCTURAL AND SERVICES ENGINEER BURO HAPPOLD
QS GLEEDS
PROJECT MANAGER GLEEDS MANAGEMENT SERVICES
LANDSCAPE ARCHITECT CHRISTOPHER BRADLEY-HOLE
CONTRACTOR BOVIS LEND LEASE
GROSS INTERNAL AREA 95,250 SQUARE METRES
CONTRACT VALUE £250 MILLION
PHOTOGRAPHERS PETER COOK – VIEW/ DENNIS GILBERT – VIEW/NICHOLAS GUTTRIDGE

EXTENSION TO PRIVATE HOUSE
.LONDON W1 .HENNING STUMMEL ARCHITECTS LTD

To make sense of this tiny house it would be almost impossible to incorporate modern bathrooms within the existing interior; their size would overwhelm the modest rooms on each floor. The original eighteenth-century design could not have anticipated modern bathing requirements, so a separate rear extension is entirely logical. It is equally logical, and in keeping with good conservation practice, that the tiny extension should clearly articulate its difference from the historic structure.

Unfortunately, modesty and logic get you nowhere with the Leviathan of planning bureaucracy. The whole weight of Westminster's planning department was brought to bear on Henning's little garden jakes. Despite negotiations, meetings, compromises and witty reinventions, planning consent was refused. The architect appealed to the secretary of state for the environment. At last a window of sanity opened, and the appeal inspector confirmed that this little loo caused no offence. The waste of time, money and resources doesn't bear thinking about.

The extension is a wooden tower with clapboard walls. It is attached to the house at each level. The planners insisted that any window must be traditional in style, so the architect got rid of windows altogether. Tiny slats of opalescent Perspex illuminate the interior. The inside glows by day and the outside has a Morse code of light dots and dashes by night. Each little room has an intricate arrangement of secret cabinets, folding doors and Perspex panels. It feels like a lively reinvention of an eighteenth-century house.

It is good to see a young designer experimenting on himself. Some of his ideas have not worked as intended; the Perspex slats will be difficult to clean, but it is his house and he will find a way to clean them. Some of the workmanship is thin. Perhaps the time and money wasted in overcoming the planning labyrinth could more usefully have been spent on builders and better materials. What has been achieved is remarkably light and elegant and funny. It is a triumph of wit and invention over deadening bureaucracy.

CLIENTS HENNING AND BEATRICE STUMMEL
STRUCTURAL ENGINEER MICHAEL HADI ASSOCIATES
CONTRACTOR PNK CONTRACTS
GROSS INTERNAL AREA 15 SQUARE METRES
CONTRACT VALUE £60,000
PHOTOGRAPHERS NIGEL RIGDEN/ LUKE CAULFIELD

SHORTLISTED FOR THE STEPHEN LAWRENCE PRIZE

FACULTY BUILDING, IMPERIAL COLLEGE
.LONDON SW7 .FOSTER AND PARTNERS

This, the fourth commission for Foster and Partners at Imperial College, brings together all the college's key administrative staff for the first time.

The first reaction to this ink-blue building, with its apparent simplicity of form, is a mix of shock and pleasant surprise. The impact of its strong colour and simple geometry goes a long way towards humanizing an otherwise dreary and – in both senses of the word – pedestrian space. Furthermore, the interaction of the block with the ramp slicing through its corner, and the latter's role as entrance, create complexity benefiting both building and space.

The glazing and cladding exhibit a welcome sensuality previously absent from ubiquitous all-glass assemblies. The cladding consists of apparently randomly distributed opaque panels in three shades of blue. A significant share of the credit here belongs to the collaborating artist, the Dane Per Arnoldi. One can also attribute to Arnoldi the exploitation of the light-catching capability of glass. Strong orange-coloured columns follow the line of the ramp and are read through the blue glass panels, further enlivening the façade.

The interior is physically and visually comfortable, benefiting to some extent from the floorplate geometry of the diagonal cut and, of course, the environmentally friendly provisions. Warmth is provided by waste heat from the heat-and-power plant serving the whole campus. Chilled beams provide cooling. And the architects have used recycled timber and plastic to make up the surface of the deck. The upper floors overlie car and cycle parking spaces (30 cars and 600 bikes – enough for the entire campus), hidden from the precinct view by the change of level, which generates the ramp.

The quality of the design and the innovative move of the ramp point to a richer architecture, and earn recognition for the scheme as a whole.

CLIENT IMPERIAL COLLEGE LONDON
INTEGRATED ENGINEERING BURO HAPPOLD
PROJECT MANAGEMENT GARDINER & THEOBALD MANAGEMENT
SERVICES, HEALTH & SAFETY JENKINS & POTTER
ACOUSTIC ENGINEERING SANDY BROWN ASSOCIATES
CONTRACTOR EXTERIOR PLC
GROSS INTERNAL AREA 4800 SQUARE METRES
CONTRACT VALUE £10 MILLION
PHOTOGRAPHER NIGEL YOUNG

GROUND-FLOOR PLAN

FRIENDSHIP HOUSE
.LONDON SE1 .MACCORMAC JAMIESON PRICHARD

When viewed from the railway, Friendship House presents a wall of zinc shingles punctuated by tiny peephole windows. It provides a welcome contrast to its drab surroundings and invites further inspection to find out what lies behind the wall.

It turns out to be a hostel for 160 young working people and students, and it performs this function very well. The accommodation is wrapped around the edge of an irregular site, with a well-landscaped garden court providing a focus. The courtyard has a pool and fountain to reflect light back into the complex, and their gentle white noise counters that of the railway and surrounding streets. The gated entrance area makes this a secure environment, particularly suitable for newcomers to London.

Inside, the space is detailed to a high standard. There is a mix of communal areas, kitchen spaces for groups of eight to ten, and individual (with some double) study bedrooms. It feels a bit like a college residence out of context. There are also nine rooms designed for residents with physical disabilities. The en-suite bathrooms were prefabricated as pods off site.

The development is superbly insulated from the adjacent railway (none of the rooms overlooks the tracks) and feels very secure. It sits on vibration pads to absorb movement from passing trains. However, as a model for future city living, the inevitable security gate and perimeter fence pose questions about the conflicting needs of safety and integration with the community.

The tightness of the site is relieved by a strong diagonal part-internal and part-external route linking the communal parts of the building. This feature is exaggerated by clever lighting and visually extended by mirrors placed at either end.

CLIENT LONDON HOSTELS ASSOCIATION
STRUCTURAL ENGINEER BUTLER & YOUNG ASSOCIATES
SERVICES ENGINEER MICHAEL POPPER ASSOCIATES
QS TRINICK TURNER
CONTRACTOR GALLIFORD TRY PARTNERSHIPS
GROSS INTERNAL AREA 4810 SQUARE METRES
CONTRACT VALUE £7.47 MILLION
PHOTOGRAPHER PETER DURANT – ARCBLUE.COM

HOME OFFICE HEADQUARTERS
.LONDON SW1 .TERRY FARRELL & PARTNERS

The new Home Office Headquarters in Marsham Street represents a quiet piece of urbanism. Although it is a PFI-delivered scheme, the impressive screen by Liam Gillick that gives the façade its character has survived the close attentions of the value engineers. The building represents the culmination of some fourteen years of masterplanning, design proposals and construction. The site, in the centre of London and close to the Houses of Parliament, is an important one and the scale of the new development is such that the new building is a feature of considerable significance in the area.

The building addresses and solves many of the deficiencies of the previous (Department of the Environment) buildings on the site. While maintaining density, it is relatively low (five to seven storeys), similar in height and massing to the surrounding buildings. It improves the public realm at street level with generous landscaped spaces and by restoring 'side streets' as pedestrian links that make the site more permeable. The introduction of a residential building along one edge of the site (presumably a planning requirement) gives the development a mixed-use component.

The external architecture makes a significant contribution to the streetscape. Every effort has been made to compensate for the severe constraints imposed by the security needs of the brief (no shops or cafés to give 'active' façades). Public art in the form of coloured-glass vitrines, façade typography, sculpture and coloured canopies, as well as high-quality materials and landscaping features (water, trees, grassed areas) give life to the architecture and the public spaces around the building. The entrance area, with its set-back space, high canopy and the grand scale of the elevation, is impressive.

Internally, the building feels pleasant and comfortable. Atriums within the office floorplates bring daylight into the heart of the working areas. The central atrium gives the building a 'community' space with informal areas that promote social interaction. The open-plan office spaces, while conventional, are of high quality and seem to be popular with their civil-servant users.

CLIENT ANNES GATE PROPERTY
ARCHITECT, MASTERPLANNER AND PRINCIPAL INTERIORS TERRY FARRELL & PARTNERS
ARTIST LIAM GILLICK
STRUCTURAL ENGINEER PELL FRISCHMANN
MECHANICAL ENGINEER BATTLE MCCARTHY
ELECTRICAL ENGINEER FLACK & KURTZ
LANDSCAPE ARCHITECT LOVEJOY
OFFICE INTERIORS DEGW
CONTRACTOR BOUYGUES UK LTD
GROSS INTERNAL AREA 71,830 SQUARE METRES
CONTRACT VALUE £311 MILLION
PHOTOGRAPHER RICHARD BRYANT – ARCAID

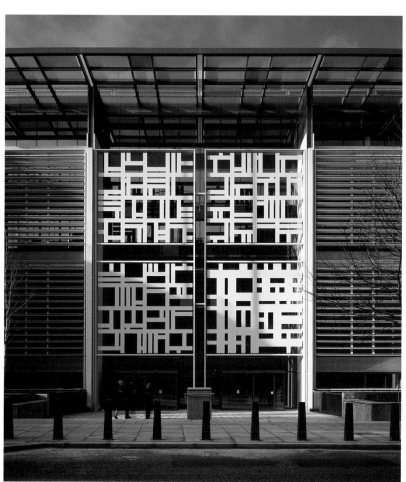

IDEA STORE CHRISP STREET
.LONDON E14 .ADJAYE ASSOCIATES

David Adjaye's Idea Store is the second in a series of seven commissioned by Tower Hamlets, offering internet access, books, CDs and DVDs, as well as lifelong-learning courses. The building uses coloured glass as an electronic billboard and video wall. As a public building, it is positioned appropriately in the middle of a small shopping centre, clearly visible from East India Dock Road, and built above a single-storey parade of shops.

The building is easy to understand and is clearly much liked and well used. Internet facilities and general information desks are located next door to the entrance on the ground floor, with lifts, staircase and a one-way escalator directing visitors to the library and study rooms on the first floor. Here, the long reading-room combines an inventive system of serpentine bookcases below eye level and study spaces. This room achieves a sense of inclusiveness and, without recourse to populist tricks, is very popular.

The building makes little concession to its context. Sitting directly above a nondescript parade of shops, it abuts a banal concrete bridge/deck, backs on to an equally unmemorable service building, and so on, without mediation. Rather than make ingratiating gestures to 'improving' existing buildings, its unbridled newness carries a strong message of regeneration and social potency.

CLIENT LONDON BOROUGH OF TOWER HAMLETS
ENGINEERING SERVICES ARUP
FAÇADE CONSULTANT ARUP FAÇADE ENGINEERING
GRAPHIC DESIGN MODE
CONTRACTOR VERRY CONSTRUCTION
GROSS INTERNAL AREA 1300 SQUARE METRES
CONTRACT VALUE £2.3 MILLION
PHOTOGRAPHERS LYDON DOUGLAS/ TIM SOAR

MOSSBOURNE COMMUNITY ACADEMY
.LONDON E5 .RICHARD ROGERS PARTNERSHIP

Mossbourne Community Academy is one of the government's new public–private partnership schools, with a large lump-sum benefaction coming from a rich individual (in this case Sir Michael Wilshaw) who helps drive the project and sits on the board of governors. (Another of these schools, The Business Academy Bexley, reached last year's Stirling Prize shortlist.) Each academy has a specialism: in this case information and communication technology. It is not just about the curriculum, the teaching environment is also a focus, so there are some big architectural names involved, too: last year's academy was by Foster, this is by Rogers.

This building proposes a radical rethink of the physical setting for secondary education. It embodies the relationships between teachers and students proposed in the brief, and it is a vivid example of the benefits of collaboration between client and architect. It replaces what was often described, not least by the Tory government, as the worst school in Britain, Hackney Downs, which closed in 1995.

The perimeter wall protects the school from its harsh environment – railway lines enclose two sides of the triangular site – and engenders a sense of community. The school is organized around three-storey subject-based houses, each with its own vertical circulation and local staff centres. More than one student said that this organization, and the general openness of the corridors, prevented bullying.

The quality of the interior, robust but bright and cheerful, is a triumph. The oversized timber structure – one of the biggest in the country – is an enjoyably reassuring presence, and the toplit information and communication technology suites provide a focus for each house. The school is optimistic in its intellectual outlook, aspiring to accessibility, openness and social inclusion. The architecture reflects this: across its playground it faces one of the best things about Hackney (still the most deprived London borough), Hackney Downs.

CLIENT MOSSBOURNE TRUST
STRUCTURAL ENGINEER WHITBYBIRD
SERVICES ENGINEER BDSP
LANDSCAPE ARCHITECT KINNEAR LANDSCAPE ARCHITECTS
CONTRACTOR MACE LTD
CONTRACT VALUE £23 MILLION
GROSS INTERNAL AREA 8312 SQUARE METRES
PHOTOGRAPHER DAVID CHURCHILL

NEIGHBOURHOOD NURSERY + CHILDREN'S CENTRE
.HOUNSLOW .COTTRELL + VERMEULEN
ARCHITECTURE

This prototype nursery provides facilities for the under-fives – as well as training for their parents – in a series of colourful prefabricated units under an over-arching roof, which also produces cover for play areas on terraces and internal courts, including a deep sand-pit.

In a northern climate the transition between outdoor and indoor space is fraught with problems. In a nursery where children are living for much of the day and, in winter, for almost all of the daylight hours, the issue is critical to the ambience and sense of freedom felt by small children and their carers. The triumph of this building is its handling of the crucial junction between inside and out.

The Neighbourhood Nursery is pioneering in the way that it takes on this issue holistically and manages greatly to expand the internal spaces into fresh-air spaces that are dry and luminous. It does so by erecting a separate rainscreen roof that extends beyond the single-storey children's accommodation below (an interesting alternative to Will Alsop's solution at Fawood). Sadly, the architect's original proposal for using a lightweight French framing for this over-arching element could not be realized, and the substituted British steel frame is over-heavy for its purpose.

The rooms, organized for different age activities, all make use of the adjacent outside rooms. Rather than being isolated events, these deep porch areas are interconnected in various ways to create a really exciting landscape under the translucent roof. The gardens are defined by low sturdy timber fences and gates, and these continue outside the structure into small fields with prairie-style planting and existing mature cherry trees. The advantages of a generous suburban plot are fully exploited by creating tame and wild play spaces.

At one magical point the plain interior space is opened up beneath the outer roof to create a sheltered courtyard filled with clean, white sand so deep that it drains naturally.

CLIENT NATIONAL DAY NURSERIES ASSOCIATION
PROJECT MANAGER HIVES ASSOCIATES
STRUCTURAL ENGINEER HASKINS ROBINSON WATERS
SERVICES ENGINEER MAX FORDHAM LLP
CONTRACTOR DURKAN PUDELEK
CONTRACT VALUE £1.3 MILLION
GROSS INTERNAL AREA 750 SQUARE METRES
PHOTOGRAPHER PETER GRANT

PLAN

THE ORANGERY, GREAT ORMOND STREET HOSPITAL .LONDON WC1 .SPACELABUK

The Orangery is a piece of serendipity dropped into the heart of Great Ormond Street Hospital. The site is the boiler-house roof, flanked on one side by a coffee shop and on the other by the staff canteen, overlooked on all sides by the hospital. The brief was for a 'conservatory-type building' to provide both an internal and an external area for eating and drinking. It was to be different from a 'normal hospital canteen experience' and could be used for functions, presentations and exhibitions as well as entertaining.

The design is generated by broad bands of timber and resin running the length of the site. These turn up to form a wall containing the space at the western end, but turn up and over to create an enclosure at the eastern end. The potential of this volume is developed in a sculptural way with the bands adopting different geometries and curving up and down over the roof plane. The exterior of the Orangery is clad in zinc and the façade to the courtyard is simply glazed, as are the vertical spaces. Access is by ramp from the coffee shop and by a short flight of stairs from the canteen. The orthogonal nature of the courtyard is enlivened by recessed lighting and timber planters, which also provide enclosure to smaller areas of seating. When viewed from above, the Orangery and its courtyard occupy their space confidently, acknowledging the fact that the roof is another façade to be considered and appreciated.

The Orangery was built in just twenty-four weeks (the steel structure was prefabricated off-site and craned in) and is remarkably good value for money. It is well used by staff and visitors and a measure of its success is that consultants, who had not previously used the coffee shop, do so now. The client intends to use the same approach in other courtyard areas. Exemplary in the way it uses gash space – an unused and unloved roof area – the scheme creates a facility at once exciting and tranquil. This is architecture as therapy – like the Maggie's Centres – and both architect and client deserve equal credit for it.

CLIENT GREAT ORMOND STREET HOSPITAL
STRUCTURAL ENGINEER RODRIGUES ASSOCIATES
LANDSCAPE CONSULTANT EARTHSCAPE
CONTRACTOR GRANVILLE BUILDING CO.
GROSS INTERNAL AREA 70 SQUARE METRES
CONTRACT VALUE £390,000
PHOTOGRAPHER JEFFERSON SMITH

SHORTLISTED FOR THE STEPHEN LAWRENCE PRIZE

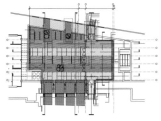

PEABODY LOW-COST HOUSING
.LONDON E16 .NIALL MCLAUGHLIN ARCHITECTS

Silvertown is the land of the 'Juliet balcony': a strangely suburban village where all the buildings are clad in the cheapest and lightest London stock brick. It is therefore a relief to find, in the middle of this sprawl, the jewel that is Evelyn Road.

This housing project, consisting of twelve apartments, was built for the Peabody Trust, RIBA Client of the Year in 2004. They chose Niall McLaughlin through a competition process where the aim was to find smaller architectural firms with inventive solutions for low-cost housing. The client also encouraged the inclusion of an artist on the team.

The low-cost modular timber-frame apartments have two bedrooms and a living-room. The massing is broken down into three larger blocks, which helps to delineate clearly the two entrances. So far so conventional, but instead of using brick, timber, or tiles the entrances are wrapped in a coloured film, chosen by artist Martin Richman, that produces iridescent shifting patterns like a peacock's feathers. The frontage is made up of glazed planks lined in a dichroic film and fitted into double-glazed units. The resulting effect is both dazzling and dynamic; the colour of the fully glazed façade changes constantly with the movement of the sun. This façade is opaque, which, given its externally translucent nature, is a slight surprise. Instead, windows are located internally on corners to offer long views along the streets. The rear and side façades, clad in painted timber, are carefully composed and well detailed.

The flats themselves are well planned, with generous living-rooms/kitchens. Each two-bedroom apartment has either a balcony or an outdoor terrace. The communal staircases are clad in plywood, while exposed conduits supply the lighting. Perhaps what is most interesting about Evelyn Road is that its basic model could be applied on a much larger scale. In an area of outstanding architectural mediocrity Evelyn Street offers the mass housebuilders, whose schemes surround this project, a viable and inventive way forward.

CLIENT PEABODY TRUST
STRUCTURAL ENGINEER WHITBYBIRD
ARTIST MARTIN RICHMAN
PROJECT MANAGER WALKER MANAGEMENT
CONTRACTOR SANDWOOD CONSTRUCTION
GROSS INTERNAL AREA 1200 SQUARE METRES
CONTRACT VALUE £1.5 MILLION
PHOTOGRAPHER NICHOLAS KANE

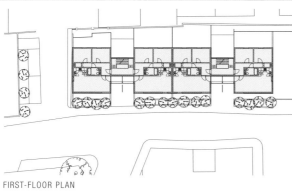

FIRST-FLOOR PLAN

171 .LONDON

PETER JONES
.LONDON SW1 .JOHN MCASLAN + PARTNERS

Peter Jones is one of a triumvirate of Modernist masterpieces in London that, having been the subjects of sympathetic restoration, have received RIBA Awards this year (see pp. 50 and 176).The quality of the seamless restoration and improvements to this icon of pre-war Modernity makes an obvious impact. It is evident that this highly sensitive, daring and complex intervention was entered into with an unusual degree of respect for the existing building, and in a gratifying collaboration with the enthusiastic owner–client. Of course, this enthusiasm was bolstered by the fact that the amount of retail space was being increased. But responsibility for the fact that the store was able to remain open throughout the extensive rebuild was freely attributed to the design team as well as the contractors.

The Grade II-listed store's sinuous curtain wall, one of the first in London, disguised a series of internal problems, because the structure is an amalgam of several buildings with floor heights that did not easily relate to each other. The most significant structural work therefore involved the harmonization of floor levels and the introduction of a seven-storey atrium that creates a dramatic focus for the complex and aids orientation. This new space, replacing a smaller existing lightwell, is capped with a rooftop restaurant with spectacular views over London. Climate control has been improved throughout the building and retail space increased by 20%.

Inherent in restoration projects is the reasonable and defendable attribution of credit between the original and the restoring architects. This project poses few problems in this respect, and the restoring architects' sensitivity, taste and conscientiousness in attention to detail and high professionalism has produced an exemplary outcome. The result is the conservation of – and indeed improvement to – a significant piece of architectural heritage.

CLIENT JOHN LEWIS PARTNERSHIP
STRUCTURAL ENGINEER HIRST PEIRCE & MALCOLM
SERVICES ENGINEER TROUP BYWATERS & ANDERS
QS DAVIS LANGDON
PLANNING CONSULTANT F.D.P. SAVILL
EXECUTIVE ARCHITECT BAMBER & REDDAN
CONTRACTOR BOVIS LEND LEASE
GROSS INTERNAL AREA 30,000 SQUARE METRES
CONTRACT VALUE £100 MILLION
PHOTOGRAPHER PETER COOK – VIEW

SHORTLISTED FOR THE RIBA INCLUSIVE DESIGN AWARD

GROUND-FLOOR PLAN

PRIOR WESTON SCHOOL, TEMPORARY ACCOMMODATION
.LONDON EC1 .PENOYRE & PRASAD LLP

A temporary building would not normally be considered for an architecture prize, but this one is a triumph of good sense and the responsible use of money, aided by a palpable enthusiasm for the project. Built in just six weeks in the summer holiday (three of the classrooms were erected in a weekend), it has transformed a collection of tired mid-twentieth-century school units into a vibrant, bright and fully integrated school.

The heart of the old school was a central IT and library space. The architects have cleverly re-created the spirit of this place by enclosing the central area between three existing blocks with a new building at the front of the site. This lends the school a new presence on the street, and is lifted by the treatment given to it by artist and parent Sian Tucker working with children from the school. The new foyer building is top-lit and is an open and energetic space housing reception, library, administration and an open-sided classroom.

The enthusiasm of the headmistress for the project was clearly important, and the result has transformed a mix of architectural parts into an entirely coherent and cheerful environment, in which each difficulty has been seen as an opportunity for invention. Notable in this regard are the office of the headmistress, cunningly discovered within an enticing blue plastic corral, and the disabled ramp, which has been transformed into a much-loved part of the playground.

This is a seriously experimental building. The new units are made of engineered prefabricated timber-framed wall, while the floor and roof cassettes are based on a plywood-sheet module. Because there was no time for concrete foundations (nor could they be justified in terms of sustainability for so short a life), the cassettes rest on strip foundations no deeper than the topsoil. The building is designed to be recycled when it is replaced by a permanent school in three years. The school family will be sorry to see it go.

CLIENT LONDON BOROUGH OF ISLINGTON
STRUCTURAL ENGINEER ALAN CONISBEE AND ASSOCIATES
ARTIST SIAN TUCKER
PROJECT MANAGER DEVELOPING PROJECTS
PLANNING SUPERVISOR TMP LTD
CONTRACTOR FRAMEWORK CDM
GROSS INTERNAL AREA 480 SQUARE METRES
CONTRACT VALUE £629,600
PHOTOGRAPHER R.A.F. MAKDA – VIEW

GROUND PLAN

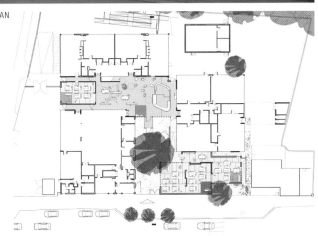

PRIVATE HOUSE
.LONDON NW6 .AVANTI ARCHITECTS LTD

This Grade II*-listed house was designed by Colin Lucas of Connell, Ward and Lucas in 1938. Before listing, the house had been altered in a number of respects, the principal ones being the incorporation of a swimming pool at ground level and a master-bedroom suite in the the rooftop covered terrace.

It was not at all what the clients were looking for, but the man, at least, immediately fell in love with it. His wife took a little more persuading, given that it had not been well maintained and had deteriorated badly. The brief to the architect was to design and specify a full scheme of repair, upgrade and alteration works to provide a high-quality house well-equipped to current standards.

The original fabric has been repaired where possible; new work matches the old and the building has been recoated in its original colours. With the agreement of English Heritage, the design has rebuilt the post-war alterations made to the building in a manner deemed sympathetic to the original Lucas design; the swimming-pool volume now sits happily within the composition of the rear façade. The materials used throughout are of high quality and the detailing of new works does not try to replicate that of the original.

The jury agreed that new work should be honestly expressed, rather than pastiching the old, so the question was whether its quality matched that of the original. They looked in particular at the work carried out in the master-bedroom suite and at the columns in the living-room, which are based on a feature in another house of the period. In the end they overcame their worries about the inclusion of a feature from another Modernist architect and concluded that it was well designed and executed. A model, in fact, for taking a classic house of one century and making it work in the next.

CLIENT PRIVATE
CLIENT AGENT LANDER AND COMPANY
STRUCTURAL ENGINEER ALAN CONISBEE AND ASSOCIATES
SERVICES ENGINEER MARTIN THOMAS ASSOCIATES
LANDSCAPE ARCHITECT LOUDA DESIGN LTD
LANDSCAPE CONTRACTOR STEPHEN BAXTER
CONTRACTOR GLENNINGS LTD
GROSS INTERNAL AREA 392 SQUARE METRES
CONTRACT VALUE £1.4 MILLION
PHOTOGRAPHERS NICHOLAS KANE/ JOHN ALLEN

ST MARY'S GARDEN HALL
.LONDON SW19 .TERRY PAWSON ARCHITECTS

St Mary's Garden Hall is an attractively modest insertion into a sensitive, well-cared for conservation area, close by the Grade II-listed nineteenth-century St Mary's Church. The scheme – typical of this thoughtful practice – involves a reinterpretation of the materials traditionally associated with ecclesiastical buildings.

The building is in itself of high architectural quality. And paradoxically, by avoiding being 'in keeping', the adventurous design manages to create formal and material counterpointing to enhance both the existing and the new buildings. Stated concerns for scale are successfully addressed by careful adjustments of floor and roof levels, and the use of unfashionable flat roofs.

The building's simple but sophisticated geometry is nicely underwritten by juxtaposed planes of white limestone, translucent glass and unostentatious timber elements, contrasting with a rough blue/brown drystone wall on the street elevation. The glazing makes up a light-bar – an element inspired by the work of the stained-glass artists of the past – and provides another counterpoint to the mass of the stonework. The hall sits in a sunken garden that becomes another room when the big glazed doors are opened up.

The interiors continue the theme of precise simplicity with the use of white-plastered walls and partitions. These are popular, well-used community spaces. The only question is whether the fabric, already showing a lack of maintenance, will stand up to the evident success of the venue.

The hall provides proof that adventurousness can survive the hazards of conservation constraints, through an understanding client body working with a sympathetic planning authority and, not least, a talented and concerned architect.

CLIENT ST MARY'S PAROCHIAL CHURCH COUNCIL
STRUCTURAL ENGINEER BARTON ENGINEERS
QS PIERCE HILL
CONTRACTOR CARDY CONSTRUCTION
GROSS INTERNAL AREA 200 SQUARE METRES
CONTRACT VALUE £496,000
PHOTOGRAPHER TOM SCOTT

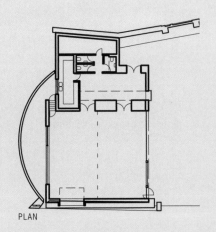

PLAN

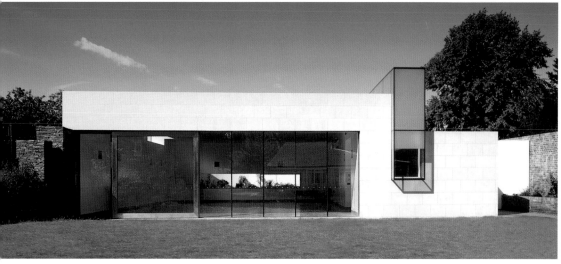

TOWER HILL ENVIRONS SCHEME .LONDON EC3 .STANTON WILLIAMS

Tower Hill is the traditional approach to the Tower of London. The improvements officially opened by the Queen in July 2004 represent the last phase of an eight-year, £20-million scheme to improve the setting of the Tower to match its status as a World Heritage site and royal palace, and to create a new space for public enjoyment. The scheme involves the provision of new ticketing facilities, a 'welcome centre', an enlarged shop, an education centre within the Tower Vaults building and the reinstallation of a historic road under its traditional name, Petty Wales.

The change in the approach to the Tower is remarkable. Replacing the somewhat jumbled collection of buildings and barriers of the past is a grandly sloping open space, from which both the Tower and the Thames are visible as never before. Instead of queues of patient visitors, there is an exhilarating open space in which people can walk, stop and sit down at will before joining the general movement of visitors down the long granite slope to the entrance.

The detailing of the new pavilions is cool and refreshing in its minimal and elegant use of steel and glass. The pavilions are themselves unfussy in outline, and establish a calm wall along the western approaches to the square. Lights, benches, signs and ticket booths all contribute to a scheme that is fresh, calm and confident in its classic simplicity.

Writing in *The Sunday Times*, Hugh Pearman said: 'Tower Hill, which used to be a confused collection of tacky buildings, kiosks and a rat-run of a road, has had a benign, ordering hand swept across it. This is architecture as landscape .... It is not just the Tower that is revealed in a new light .... This is high-quality public space – a real luxury, opening up a whole new vista even for jaded London eyes.'

CLIENT HISTORIC ROYAL PALACES
STRUCTURAL AND SERVICES ENGINEER ARUP
LIGHTING DESIGNER LAPD
QS GARDINER & THEOBOLD
DISABILITY CONSULTANT ALL CLEAR DESIGNS
ARCHAEOLOGICAL CONSULTANT KEEVIL
HERITAGE CONSULTANCY
SOFT LANDSCAPING CHURCHMAN
LANDSCAPE ARCHITECTS
CONTRACTOR WALLIS
GROSS AREA 2182 SQUARE METRES
(BUILDINGS)/8440 SQUARE METRES
(LANDSCAPE)
CONTRACT VALUE £8.8 MILLION
(BUILDINGS)/£5 MILLION (LANDSCAPE)
PHOTOGRAPHERS DENNIS GILBERT – VIEW/
MORLEY VON STERNBERG

THE WELLCOME TRUST GIBBS BUILDING
.LONDON NW1 .HOPKINS ARCHITECTS

The Wellcome Trust's brief was for an administrative building for 500 people that would provide exemplary working conditions and reflect the Trust's prestige – 'distinctive but not flashy, timeless but not extravagant'. The site, adjacent to the charity's Greek Revival headquarters, has Euston Road on its north side and the smaller scale Gower Place to the south.

The building's organization responds to the site by locating a ten-storey-high, 18-metre-deep block along the length of Euston Road and a five-storey-high, 9-metre-deep block parallel to and separated from it by a 9-metre-wide atrium, facing Gower Place. The atrium is the principal circulation route at ground floor, providing access to the lifts and stairs and ensuring that it is used by everyone, not just by people using the café. It is also home to an outstanding Thomas Heatherwick sculpture, *Bleigiessen*. Made of 150,000 coloured glass spheres suspended on one million metres of stainless-steel wire, it rises through six storeys at the building's west end.

The asymmetry of the building section is further developed with the two office zones differing in spatial organization; the deeper floorplate has internal horizontal circulation routes, two-storey voids incorporating planting or a spiral staircase and, on the lower floors, openable windows to the main atrium, while the Gower Place block has a circulation zone next to the atrium. The building's form confidently addresses Euston Road, its expressed steel structure giving an order and scale appropriate to its location. The disparity in height of the blocks is resolved by a single curved roof sweeping down and enclosing the atrium and the restaurant on the top level of the south block.

The Gibbs Building is generous in scale, engineered to provide a good internal environment and detailed consistently to the highest standard. It also provides for individual foibles – bridges are wide, balustrading made of opaque glass and half the passenger lifts are fully enclosed so that vertigo sufferers are accommodated. This exemplary approach to design and realization shows Hopkins at his very best.

CLIENT THE WELLCOME TRUST
STRUCTURAL ENGINEER WSP
SERVICES ENGINEER CUNDALL JOHNSTON & PARTNERS
CONTRACTOR MACE LTD
GROSS INTERNAL AREA 28,000 SQUARE METRES
CONTRACT VALUE £90 MILLION
PHOTOGRAPHER NICOLAS GUTTRIDGE

GROUND-FLOOR PLAN

SAMPENSION HEADQUARTERS
.COPENHAGEN, DENMARK .3XNIELSEN A/S

This new headquarters for Sampension, one of Denmark's leading pension providers, is on the site of the former Tuborg brewery. In moving from its previous building of traditional cellular offices the company wanted to promote more open and collaborative working as well as a new forward-looking image for the organization. The new building has been very successful in achieving these objectives.

The building is arranged in two parallel ranges. The front range is clad in granite, which frames glazed offices faced with vertically pivoted shutters of perforated copper. On the rear range the perforated copper continues full length, extending at each end to form gables framing horizontal fixed louvres to the south and unshaded glazing to the north. During the day the copper shutters appear to be solid when closed, with a very fine colour and texture owing to the light and shade falling on them. This will only improve with age as the copper, a vernacular roofing material in Copenhagen, turns green with verdigris. However, when the sun is reflected off the glass behind, or when the internal lights become visible after dusk, the shutters dematerialize. Moreover, since each shutter can be rotated to be open or closed by the occupant of the office, the whole appearance of the elevations is constantly changing, and the effect is very beautiful.

A generous entrance at ground level leads via a wide stair to a first-floor atrium with oval balconies and curved stairs providing circulation to the fully glazed offices and meeting rooms flanking it higher up. The glazed lifts also overlook the atrium, seen through a screen of LED tubular lighting down which water trickles at about the same speed at which the lifts move. These are lit from below and provide a calm atmosphere, contributing to the excellent working environment.

CLIENT SAMPENSION
STRUCTURAL ENGINEER RAMBØLL
CONTRACTOR NCC CONSTRUCTION DANMARK A/S
GROSS INTERNAL AREA 9500 SQUARE METRES
CONTRACT VALUE £18.5 MILLION
PHOTOGRAPHER ADAM MØRK

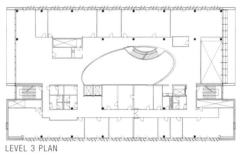

LEVEL 3 PLAN

185 .EUROPEAN UNION

MILLAU VIADUCT
.TARN VALLEY, FRANCE .FOSTER AND PARTNERS
WITH MICHEL VIRLOGEUX (ENGINEER)

In an extraordinary project, Eiffel, the great infrastructure consortium, has built a viaduct to span the Tarn valley. It flies out over a precipice, bypassing towns, rivers and a whole nature reserve. The design concept for a multispan cable-stay bridge is by Michel Virlogeux, an engineer with a hundred bridges to his credit. But his newly appointed boss wanted to make sure there were no better ideas out there, so an international competition was organized. Foster's was the concept nearest to that of Virlogeux.

The structural solution to this 2-kilometre crossing is a procession of slender concrete piers rising from the valley floor. The road bridge spanning between the piers is made like the hull of a ship. Steel ribs support a stressed-skin of steel sheet. In construction, each steel hull section was pushed out across the gap, like a suspended supertanker. Cars drive along the top surface, which acts just like a deck. In order to lengthen the span, a mast rises above each of the steel hulls. Cables are attached from the head of the masts to the hull. The steel hull, the masts and the cables form a stiff structure that is able to span from pier to pier.

Foster and Partners worked as consulting architects with the engineers on this structure. The principles of this kind of bridge would have been familiar to engineers of the heroic age of British engineering – the power of the viaduct comes from its scale more than any structural innovation. The architects have put considerable effort into tailoring important details. The transparent windguards are elegant and allow motorists to stay in touch with the landscape below. The treatment of the masts is refined and it is clear that it minimizes the bulk of the structure when seen from beneath. The 'tuning fork' profile allows light to pass through the piers and masts, reducing their visual mass. The designers have decided to make a visual connection between the steel masts above the deck and the concrete piers below, even though there is no direct structural connection, and the visual treatment confuses the legibility of the structural principle. The effect is oddly like the typical application of Gothic style to nineteenth-century railway suspension bridges to emphasize the height of the piers.

CLIENT ARRONDISSEMENT INTERDÉPARTEMENTAL DES OUVRAGES D'ART (A.I.O.A.), A75
DESIGN/BUILD/OPERATE CONCESSIONAIRE COMPANIE EIFFAGE DE VIADUC DE MILLAU (CEVM)
STRUCTURAL ENGINEERS EUROPE ÉTUDES GECTI/SERF/SOGELERG
ASSOCIATED ARCHITECTS CHAPELET-DEFOL-MOUSSEIGNE
LANDSCAPE ARCHITECT AGENCE TER
CONTRACTOR CEVM
LENGTH 2460 METRES
CONTRACT VALUE € 320 MILLION
PHOTOGRAPHERS NIGEL YOUNG/DANIEL JAMME/STÉPHANE COMPOINT

ELEVATION

ENTORY HOME
.ETTLINGEN, GERMANY .BEHNISCH, BEHNISCH & PARTNER

Entory House is the headquarters of Entory AG, a company that specializes in providing IT consultancy to banks. The workforce spends much of its time on the road with clients and the company wanted, in contrast, an informal and open-plan design for its HQ, but with a desk to which each of its people could return. Behnisch, Behnisch & Partner was chosen as the architect through an international competition.

The building's massing consists of a series of overlapping orthogonal beams that protrude and cantilever, forming an L-shaped composition around a new lake. Built on a suburban greenfield site, the landscape forms an integral part of the design and provides pleasant views and external meeting spaces. The external glazed façade is layered and highly articulated. The outer skin of the glazing is coloured in various palettes representing the wild flowers that grow on adjacent fields.

The central entrance atrium has all the signature details associated with a Behnisch building, where all of the key elements – balustrading, rooflights, reception furniture, staircases – are handled with great flair and colourful invention.

The fit-out of the naturally ventilated office space, with its exposed concrete ceilings, is well mannered. All of it is open-plan with a great deal of flexible break-out space, while all meeting rooms are separated by glazed screens that give a light and airy atmosphere to the workplace.

This is a quiet and sustainable model for suburban office buildings. It also shows that a corporate HQ building can be both informal and delightful.

CLIENT LVM LEBENSVERSICHERUNGEN
STRUCTURAL ENGINEER BUSCHLINGER & PARTNER GMBH
SERVICES ENGINEER INGENIEURBÜRO SCHULER
LANDSCAPE ARCHITECT STÖTZER UND NEHER GMBH
ENERGY CONCEPT PLANUNGSBÜRO DR DIPPEL
GROSS INTERNAL AREA 10,845 SQUARE METRES
CONTRACT VALUE €11.4 MILLION
PHOTOGRAPHER CHRISTIAN KANDZIA

ROUND-FLOOR PLAN

GOVERNMENT DISTRICT FIRE AND POLICE STATION .BERLIN, GERMANY .SAUERBRUCH HUTTON ARCHITECTS

Many new fire and police stations are being commissioned in Britain, mostly through the Private Finance Initiative. While bodies such as the RIBA and CABE are trying to raise design standards, too often the resulting buildings are mediocre at best. It is inspiring to see how it is done in Germany. In this instance, the external design is so unconventional that the last thing you would think it would be is something as utilitarian as a fire or police station.

The brief included combining fire and police stations in one shared facility by extending a five-storey railway building (latterly used as a tax office) dating from 1907. The design strategy is very simple: a new multicoloured three-storey extension bolts on to the rear of the existing building.

By its nature, the brief demands cellular accommodation offering few substantial architectural opportunities internally, but wherever possible the architects have made the most of these limitations. In particular there is careful attention to detail in spaces such as the officers' mess area, the prison cells and the grand staircase down to the fire appliances. The renovation works to the existing building are handled calmly with a subdued palette of colours, and within much of the new office space the external brick skin of the existing building is evident.

The new skin is the most dynamic element, consisting of a horizontal glazed rainscreen that randomly varies in colour from green to red, reflecting the liveries of the police and fire brigade respectively. From a distance these colours appear blurred and unified, while close up the individual hues become more differentiated.

Perhaps the greatest achievement of the architects is the character they have conferred on a building type that can all too often be intimidating or institutional. It shows how civic buildings can be designed with great skill and design flair to provide a truly modern community amenity.

CLIENT THE SENATE OF BERLIN
STRUCTURAL ENGINEER ARUP GMBH
PROJECT MANAGER GMS ARCHITEKTEN UND BERATENDE INGENIEURE
ENVIRONMENTAL ENGINEER PBR PLANUNGSBÜRO ROHLING AG
CONTRACTORS SCHÄLERBAU BERLIN GMBH/M&V GMBH
GROSS INTERNAL AREA 6850 SQUARE METRES
CONTRACT VALUE €12.4 MILLION
PHOTOGRAPHER BITTER + BREDT

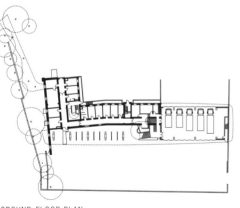

GROUND-FLOOR PLAN

91 .EUROPEAN UNION

ATHLONE CIVIC CENTRE, LIBRARY AND CENTRAL SQUARE
.ATHLONE, IRELAND .KEITH WILLIAMS ARCHITECTS

The Civic Centre and Central Square is the key project in the regeneration of Athlone's historic heart. The Centre houses the public library, the civic chamber, the secretariat and an interface with the public. Athlone has for long been an architecture-free zone (this is the place that not long ago pulled down a 1930s cinema by Royal Gold Medal-winner Michael Scott), so a good building was long overdue.

A driving force behind the scheme was the idea of providing a one-stop shop for all council services, in line with the Irish government's 'Better Local Government' initiative. The architect wanted to do a contemporary take on the heavy masonry of St Peter and Paul's Church, the Shannon Bridge and Athlone Castle. So the new centre sits on a podium overlooking the square, where concrete and teak benches humanize this monumental urban space. The entrance is dramatic, with full-height glazing recessed in the white Techcrete frame and a single set of revolving doors. Inside, to the left of the atrium is a double-height public library with offices above; to the right across a terrazzo floor is the one-stop shop, with the council chamber directly above, reached up a wide ceremonial staircase. The front elevation, which faces south, has been provided with sunshades to reduce glare. Instead of looking like clip-ons, these appear more like slits in a concrete wall.

The scheme is a public building of considerable elegance and even grandeur, but it also expresses humanity and a real sense of public accessibility and ownership. Among the features the judges particularly admired were the interior 'tribune' or public-address balcony within the lobby; the glass screen that retracts to open the civic chamber directly on to the public square; and the staircase linking the rear, basement-level children's library with the main library on the ground floor.

The intended urban sequence linking the church and its Jacobean tower with the Civic Centre and the High Street is incomplete; however, the square itself creates a pleasing, inviting and robust foreground to this commanding new building.

CLIENTS ATHLONE TOWN COUNCIL/ WESTMEATH COUNTY COUNCIL
STRUCTURAL AND M&E ENGINEER ARUP
QS DAVIS LANGDON PKS
HISTORIC BUILDINGS CONSULTANT JOHN REDMILL ARCHITECT
LIGHTING DESIGNER SUTTON VANE ASSOCIATES
CONTRACTOR JOHN SISK & SONS LTD
GROSS INTERNAL AREA 4200 SQUARE METRES
CONTRACT VALUE €15.6 MILLION
PHOTOGRAPHER EAMONN O'MAHONY

WHEATFIELD COURTYARD
.MALAHIDE, IRELAND .DAVID MCDOWELL

David McDowell has taken one of the abandoned farmhouses that still abound in rural Ireland and created a new house that has much to say about the reuse of country buildings. Traditionally, lax planning laws have meant rural Ireland is covered with a rash of mediocre (at best) new houses that pay no respect to the local vernacular or even to good taste. They are low-density, land-hungry and threaten to turn the countryside into thinly spread suburbs. More recently a tightening of regulations has meant it is almost impossible to build at all in much of the countryside. The additions to Wheatfield Courtyard signal a way out of the problem, in that they fit well into their landscape but are striking in their use of materials and volumes: Western red cedar, exposed galvanized-steel structure, floor-to-ceiling glazing.

Two stone buildings set at right angles have been converted, with new windows. They have been linked by a glass, cedar and galvanized-steel box that relates to the different levels of the two existing buildings. From this box, another projects west, offering views of the landscape, while the old buildings look in to the old farmyard. The lightness of the new structures contrasts well with the mass of the existing stone buildings, and new and old materials have been handled equally dextrously.

With its subtle blend of old and new, Wheatfield Courtyard is a fresh and sustainable answer to the problem of reconciling housing and landscape.

CLIENT DAVID MCDOWELL
STRUCTURAL ENGINEER BRIAN MCDOWELL
STRUCTURAL & CIVIL ENGINEERS
CONTRACTOR JAMES ELLIOT
CONSTRUCTION LTD
GROSS INTERNAL AREA 915 SQUARE
METRES
CONTRACT VALUE €525,000
PHOTOGRAPHER GERRY O'LEARY

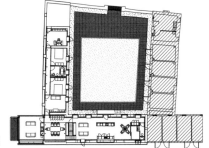

95 .EUROPEAN UNION

GROUND-FLOOR PLAN

CAFHÈ MANGIAREBERE WINE BAR .CATANIA, SICILY .STUDIO MARIA GIUSEPPINA GRASSO CANNIZZO

This bar is the work of an interesting practice based in a small south-Sicilian town, and founded by a serious architect, Maria Giuseppina Grasso Cannizzo. She has gathered around her four young architects who add energy and fresh thinking to the sophistication of her ideas. They choose to work away from the major cities, finding clients – mainly for homes or summer residences – hungry for good design in what is largely an architectural desert.

Catania is a buzzing but down-at-heel university city where 10,000 derelict projects await a practice such as this. The bar is in what was the hub of the city in the 1970s, but the university has drained the life towards the old quarter. With designer-furniture and clothes shops round the corner, Paolo, the client, is countering that trend and has now indulged a lifetime ambition to own a bar. And what a bar. The idea – common to most of this practice's projects – is the box. This one is dropped into the triangular double-height space, but pushed out into the street and clad in ceramic tiles patterned with a tapestry design common in late-nineteenth-century houses in these parts and produced nearby. In photographs they appear kitsch, but to the eye they have a vibrancy that makes one forgive, and remember.

The box is punched through to expose the inner workings of the business: bar, kitchen and, in an eyrie above, the DJ's station. The toilets, overscaled but demanded by an Italian Part M, are contained in another concrete box, an overweight version of the structural columns that support the apartments overhead. The detailing is fine: the way the red-enamelled bar top meets the tiles, the gliding full-height raw steel-framed windows, the smoothly pivoting tile-clad door – the front of the box – that you push to gain entrance. This is architecture honed to its essential elements.

The bar attracts a lively young crowd, but even after midnight and for all the hard surfaces, the acoustic is not too harsh. The architect's hand can be seen in the furnishing as well as the fit-out – from the Eames tables to the chairs designed by Björn Dahlström and made locally, and the Droog hanging lamps with their squidgy polythene shades.

CLIENT PG+R SRL
ENGINEER GIOVANNI OTTAVIANO
CONTRACTOR EDIL SPINA SNC
GROSS INTERNAL AREA 100 SQUARE METRES
CONTRACT VALUE € 155,000
PHOTOGRAPHER HÉLÈNE BINET

LAN

MAX MARA HEADQUARTERS
.REGGIO D'EMILIA, ITALY .JOHN MCASLAN
+ PARTNERS

This new campus for the Max Mara group of companies comprises five buildings set in flat farmland on the outskirts of Reggio d'Emilia. (The family-owned company still farms here and produces Parmesan cheese as well as high fashion.) The success of the project lies in the clarity of the masterplan, in the integration of landscape and buildings and in the rigour with which the buildings themselves have been executed.

The masterplan carefully manages extensive car-parking requirements in tree-lined surface areas and below the office buildings. This solution – more costly than an all-surface solution – reduces the impact of the car on the development. The main linear public open space, beautifully done by the American landscape architect Peter Walker, is the focal point of the scheme and features a rill running the length of the single-storey exhibition building. Three linked office pavilions facing it are reached by bridges. The landscaping extends to include the warehouse, a building that also accommodates an airy first-floor canteen; staff are obliged to walk in the open air to get their lunch, though umbrellas are provided for rainy days.

All the buildings use a common palette of materials and colours. They are clad mainly in terracotta, dark metal and glass. Internally, carefully detailed concrete frames and stairs are left exposed and integrated with perforated acoustic panels that include lighting and services. Like the clients' clothes, the architecture is crisp, elegant and timeless without being too challenging.

The environmental strategy of the buildings also appears to have been well considered and integrated with the structure and finishes. This includes solar shading and exposing thermal mass to reduce reliance on air-conditioning.

CLIENT MAX MARA FASHION GROUP
EXECUTIVE ARCHITECT ARCDESIGN SRL
MULTIDISCIPLINARY ENGINEER AND PROJECT MANAGER INTERTECNO SPA
LANDSCAPE ARCHITECT PETER WALKER & PARTNERS
CONTRACTORS AMBIANTE EUROPA/ FRABBONI SPA/UNIECO SCRL
GROSS INTERNAL AREA 45,000 SQUARE METRES
CONTRACT VALUE £40 MILLION
PHOTOGRAPHER MARGHERITA SPILLUTINI

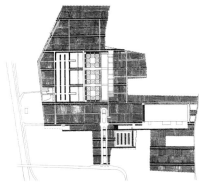

SITE PLAN

199 .EUROPEAN UNION

JAMES ROBERTSON HOUSE .GREAT MACKERAL BEACH, AUSTRALIA .DAWSON BROWN ARCHITECTURE PTY LTD

This house is an arrangement of pavilions on a narrow, elevated site overlooking the sea. Decks and steps on the steep (45-degree) slope link the pavilions. The more important rooms – kitchen/dining, sitting-room and master bedroom – sit on podiums that contain the secondary rooms and guest bedrooms. The main spaces are therefore elevated and they seem to spread out to embrace the wide views of Pittwater, Palm Beach, Barrenjoey lighthouse and the mouth of the Hawkesbury River and the ocean beyond.

The house is a series of glass, steel and copper pavilions based on a sandstone retaining wall, the whole being designed to merge into the spectacular landscape. Steel was chosen for its resistance to white ants and bushfires, as well as for its inherent strength. With its sub-tropical micro-climate and exposure to relatively little seasonal variation, the house is designed to capture on-shore breezes. Sunshading is provided by hoods, mechanical metal blinds and generous overhangs.

Australian architects seem to possess an endless supply of perfect sites, inspiring clients, temperate climates, competent builders and docile planners. Notwithstanding that, this is a beautiful house, superbly executed. It elaborates a language of perched pavilions, glazed sliding screens, fragile clerestoreys and oversailing metal roofs.

The strongest aspect of the house is the sense of framing provided by the overlapping layers of projecting eaves. This establishes a strong connection between the house and the bay beneath. It provides both shade and reflected light to the ceiling soffits. The deck between the main living-rooms looks like a special place, both protected and elevated.

CLIENTS MARCIA AND DOUGAL JAMES-ROBERTSON
ENGINEER MURTAGH BOND PTY LTD
QS DR LAWSON PTY LTD
CONTRACTOR BELLEVARDE CONSTRUCTIONS PTY LTD
LANDSCAPE BANGALLEY EARTH AND WATERSCAPES PTY LTD
GROSS INTERNAL AREA 183 SQUARE METRES
CONTRACT VALUE £820,000
PHOTOGRAPHERS PATRICK BINGHAM-HALL/ANTHONY BROWELL/ELLIOT COHEN

LOWER-FLOOR PLAN

SLICE HOUSE
.PORTO ALEGRE, BRAZIL .PROCTER : RIHL

Slice House is designed for a long narrow strip of left-over urban space, 34 metres long and only 3.4 metres wide at its narrower end, which, unsurprisingly perhaps, had been empty for more than twenty years. The client, a lecturer in her late sixties, wanted a change of lifestyle, and a new house that would look spacious and be suitable for entertaining, and be well-lit and ventilated without needing air-conditioning in the humid Brazilian climate. She believed that architecture could suggest different ways of living and preferred to spend her limited budget on interesting spaces rather than on expensive finishes.

The commission was well-timed: local government had recently relaxed planning regulations on one-off houses, concentrating instead on improving larger developer-led housing schemes. The architects have responded by providing a striking and successful solution to their stimulating brief. In-situ cast and polished or resin-coated concrete has been used for the walls and floors, with steel stairs, a steel dining and kitchen counter and aluminium windows, contributing to an appearance that is both rich and austere. The accommodation, tall and well lit, is arranged around a long courtyard garden in the middle of the site, and is fitted under roofs that slope up and down along the length of the site.

The *coup de théâtre* is the small external plunge pool that opens off the terrace at upper floor level. This has a fully glazed side that drops down into the living-room below, providing a memorable view of the swimmer to those below.

The cost of £70,000 sounds low by British standards, but £334 per square metre is average for new houses in Brazil. However, this is anything but an average house.

CLIENT NEUSA OLIVEIRA
STRUCTURAL ENGINEER MBOK, ANTONIO PASQUALI
FOUNDATION ENGINEER EDUARDO PASIN
SERVICES ENGINEER FLAVIO MAINARDI
CONTRACTOR JS CONSTRUÇOES
GROSS INTERNAL AREA 209 SQUARE METRES
CONTRACT VALUE £70,000
PHOTOGRAPHERS SUE BARR/MARCELO NUNES

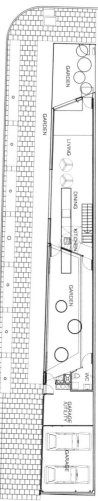

GARDEN

GARDEN

LIVING

DINING

KITCHEN

GARDEN

WC

GARAGE
/UTILITY

GARAGE

SPANISH PAVILION, EXPO 2005
.NAGOYA, JAPAN .FOREIGN OFFICE ARCHITECTS

Foreign Office Architects had a great opportunity to demonstrate their interest in cross-cultural architecture in this commission. The principle reference is to hybrid Spanish culture: a mix of Jewish-Christian and Islamic influences, in particular the courtyard with its decorative devices, lattices and traceries; and the church, with the arch and the vault.

FOA has transformed the steel box measuring 18 × 18 × 9 metres allocated to Spain by dressing it in hexagonal ceramic tiles in the colours of the Spanish flag. There are nodding references too to Spanish Caliphal and Mudejar architecture, as well as to traditional Japanese ceramic craft. The tiles are also used to form an airy screen, sheltering visitors from the heat of the Nagoya summer sun.

The pavilion is organized around a large central area that connects the seven different spaces in which the themed exhibits are to be housed. The spatial sequence is reminiscent of that which exists between a cathedral nave and its chapels, or between a courtyard and its cloisters. Here, ornate Gothic vaults, Islamic domes and faceted vaults are reinterpreted as more freeform structures containing the pavilion's different themes.

Lattices are a traditional Spanish architectural device, reflecting the fusion of Christian and Islamic architecture. The architects use them as a cladding solution for the pavilion box. The pattern is never repeated, producing a continuously varying pattern of geometry and colour. The blocks are made with glazed ceramic, a technique common on the Mediterranean Spanish coast, but also in traditional Japanese ceramics. The actual process of making a ceramic façade also literally symbolizes bringing Spanish earth to Japan.

This is a tremendously mature piece for a relatively young practice, yet it retains all the excitement and panache of its earlier work.

CLIENT SOCIEDAD ESTATAL PARA EXPOSICIONES INTERNATIONALES
STRUCTURAL ENGINEER LOW FAT STRUCTURE
M&E ENGINEER KENJI YOSHIMOTO
PROJECT MANAGER INYPSA
CONTRACTOR TAKENAKA CORPORATION NAGOYA
GROSS INTERNAL AREA 2868 SQUARE METRES
CONTRACT VALUE € 5.3 MILLION
PHOTOGRAPHER SATORU MISHIMA

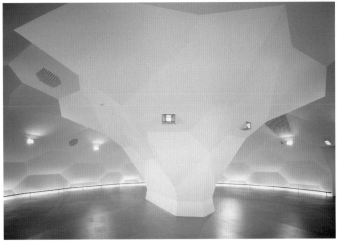

THE ESPLANADE – THEATRES ON THE BAY
.SINGAPORE .DP ARCHITECTS PTE LTD AND
MICHAEL WILFORD & PARTNERS

The Esplanade – Theatres on the Bay provides a new concert hall and theatre complex with associated front-of-house and retail areas at the heart of Singapore's civic and cultural area. On its prime waterfront site, it relates well to the context and the magnificent views in each direction.

The initial designs show Michael Wilford on top form. Traditionally, Asian cultures have designed their buildings as a rational response to the climate – something we have been painfully relearning in the West. Much of what the West has given to the East in the last century in terms of architecture – the Hongkong and Shanghai Bank being an honourable exception – ignored local conditions, depending on air-conditioning that is environmentally as well as economically expensive. Here Michael Wilford and DP Architects have found a new way of picking up on local tradition.

Particularly impressive are the glass shells and shading elements that give the architecture its distinctive form and texture. The shaping of the shells, the geometry of the varying sunshade elements as they move over the forms and the clarity of detail all contribute to an elegant and innovative solution.

Within the building, the generous interstitial spaces between the shell and the theatre/concert-hall structures provide exciting light-filled areas for visitors moving around the building, creating interesting shading patterns and giving views out over the bay. One can also understand how the building evokes a sense of traditional Asian hot-climate architecture with its clear separation and layering of shading and interior elements. The sunshade arrangement manages the difficult compromise between permitting the best views of the city and the bay while providing adequate sun protection, extremely well. In the evening the shells glow with light, transforming the building and making it appear to float.

The Esplanade building is a new landmark for Singapore – both by day and by night – and makes an important contribution to the city's contemporary civic architecture.

CLIENT THE ESPLANADE COMPANY LTD
PROJECT MANAGEMENT PM LINK PTE LTD
STRUCTURAL AND M&E ENGINEER PWD
CONSULTANTS PTE LTD (ARTS CENTRE
DEVELOPMENT DIVISION)
THEATRE CONSULTANT THEATRE PROJECT
CONSULTANTS
ACOUSTIC CONSULTANT ARTEC
CONSULTANTS INC.
CLADDING CONSULTANT ATELIER ONE
ENVIRONMENTAL ENGINEERING ATELIER TEN
CONSULTING ENGINEERS
CONTRACTOR PENTA-OCEAN
CONSTRUCTION CO. LTD
GROSS INTERNAL AREA 103,980 SQUARE
METRES
CONTRACT VALUE £200 MILLION
PHOTOGRAPHER MORI HIDETAKA

LINCOLN MODERN APARTMENTS
.SINGAPORE .SCDA ARCHITECTS PTE LTD

The thirty-storey Lincoln Modern Apartments were designed with an affluent, Westernized occupant in mind. The tower was explicitly influenced by Le Corbusier's Unité d'Habitation; in particular the concept of interlocking L-shaped volumes, which have been turned from Le Corbusier's original orientation to cross the building's façade and be legible as units from the outside. Reinforced concrete has been replaced by glazing – in a self-conscious nod to Mies – to create 'transparent glass boxes in the sky'.

The occupants of these apartments are, however, a million miles from Corbusier's collectively minded tenants. So, there are Philippe Starck bathroom fixtures, Miele kitchen appliances and timber gratings round the sunken limestone bathtubs. Apartments have 6-metre-high ceilings in the living areas and a glazed curtain wall, making them exceptionally light and airy. Over-heating is prevented by means of low-E double-glazing interstitial slits between the wall and the glass façade, creating a mild wind tunnel that draws the breeze into each room. Each apartment also features motorized shades hidden in the recesses of the ceiling to allow occupiers to control the light coming in.

Impressively, the architects have been able to adopt such a degree of Modernist rationality without straying into pastiche. The overall structure, a layered and skilfully articulated sandwich of standard components, strikingly slender and vertical, is a fresh and authentic design.

CLIENT SC GLOBAL PTE LTD
C&S ENGINEER WEB STRUCTURES
M&E ENGINEER BESCON CONSULTING ENGINEERS PTE
LANDSCAPING TIERRA DESIGN
CONTRACTOR MULTIPLEX CONSTRUCTION PTE LTD
GROSS INTERNAL AREA 6979 SQUARE METRES
CONTRACT VALUE £7.2 MILLION
PHOTOGRAPHER ALBERT LIM

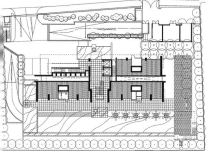

GROUND-FLOOR PLAN

SEEWURFEL
.ZURICH, SWITZERLAND .CAMENZIND EVOLUTION

Seewurfel – the word means 'lake cubes' – is a careful grouping of eight pavilions scattered across a sloping landscape near the centre of Zurich, overlooking the lake. The site, formerly industrial, has been transformed and the new development integrates happily with its surroundings, which include a neighbourhood of historic and listed buildings. Each structure is a different shape and size, and each contains both open office floors and open apartment floors, but the different uses are unified and subsumed into a holistic architectural and landscape statement.

This project demonstrates how speculative loose-fit offices and apartments can be tightly clustered in a sophisticated way to create a series of linked public piazzas. The simple, elegant fenestration appears effortlessly to link open apartments and terrace spaces over the offices. The handling of the spaces between the cubes is undogmatic and the landscape flows elegantly around and between each building block.

Mature trees are used to anchor the new project to the hillside and to provide shading. Large areas of glazing give living and working spaces views over the lake and city. Swiss standards of energy efficiency have been met using a geothermal heat pump for environmentally friendly heating and cooling. Particularly impressive is a new type of cladding panel developed for the project, in which glass is bonded to various timber-veneered MDF building boards. In this way, in addition to the richness afforded by the variously coloured timbers, the glass surface of the cladding achieves depth through random reflections of adjacent foliage, structures and the people passing by.

CLIENT SWISS LIFE
STRUCTURAL ENGINEER BASLER & HOFMANN
SERVICES ENGINEER SCHUPBACH ENGINEERING
CONTRACTOR HALTER GENERALUNTERNEHMUNG
GROSS INTERNAL AREA 12,000 SQUARE METRES
CONTRACT VALUE £25 MILLION
PHOTOGRAPHERS FERIT KUYAS/MONIKA NIKOLIC/RALPH RICHTER/REINHARD ZINDERMANN/JEAN-JACQUES RUCHTI

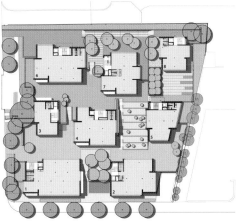

211 .WORLDWIDE

GENZYME CENTER
.CAMBRIDGE, MA, USA .BEHNISCH, BEHNISCH & PARTNER INC.

Sophisticated European architecture meets downtown US grunge on a brownfield site in Cambridge, MA. The client, a research institute, chose Behnisch to create one of the first truly environmentally aware office blocks in the US, working very consciously in a European tradition. It wanted a landmark building as a symbol of progress and to represent a point of identification for the company, its employees and visitors. The conceit of this scheme is the vertical city, with individual dwellings or workspaces and generous public areas and gardens extending through the full height of the atrium. It means people can meet by chance and chat, avoiding the sense of isolation engendered by cellular offices.

Windows are openable throughout. The building-management system opens them automatically to allow overnight cooling, but during the day the system can be over-ridden by staff. Around a third of the envelope is a double-glazed façade with a 1.22-metre interstitial space that acts as a climate buffer. Still more significantly, a climate oasis has been created by means of the gigantic daylight-flooded atrium, rising through the full twelve storeys of the building, splitting like the branches of a tree in a series of vertical, horizontal and diagonal connections – part of a sylvan boulevard that starts on the ground floor, among trees and water, and works its way up through the building, distributing light and air.

Off the route are open-plan work areas and cellular offices. These interior spaces are in the main naturally illuminated, with blinds used to filter light and deflect glare. Sun is also redirected in the atrium by means of heliostats, fixed mirrors, chandeliers and a reflective light-wall.

As well as acting as a light-chute, the atrium does much of the work of the building's climate-control system, acting as a giant chimney, drawing fresh air in through the windows and pushing it up and out at roof level. The building's energy requirements are all met by a small local power station just two blocks away. More than 75% of the building materials use recycled content, and more than half of them are locally sourced.

CLIENTS GENZYME CORPORATION AND LYME PROPERTIES
STRUCTURAL ENGINEER BURO HAPPOLD
CONTRACTOR TURNER CONSTRUCTION
GROSS INTERNAL AREA 32,500 SQUARE METRES
CONTRACT VALUE $140 MILLION
PHOTOGRAPHERS ROLAND HALBE/ANTON GRASSL/STEFAN BEHNISCH

SECOND-FLOOR PLAN

213 .WORLDWIDE

MAPS, LISTS AND SPONSORS

SCOTLAND (RIAS)

2 3   1

NORTH   10
             11

ULSTER (RSUA) 4, 5

NORTH-WEST
      8

YORKSHIRE

12, 13

9
  6
7

14

EAST MIDLANDS
        19

WEST MIDLANDS
        17
                18   24

WALES
(RSAW)   21–23
      16
                              EAST

                27   29
                      30   20   LONDON, SEE
                                          PAGES 218–19

15
                        SOUTH
26   SOUTH-EAST
        28   31   33
25   38 34
        32   36 35   37
SOUTH-WEST   WESSEX

217 .LOCATIONS

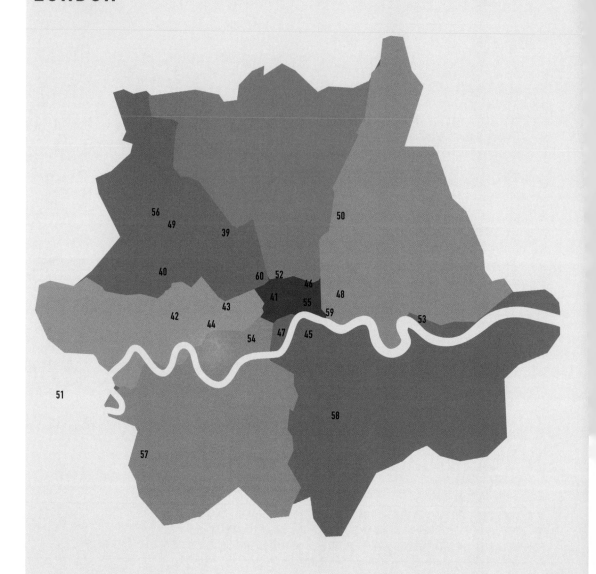

PREVIOUS WINNERS

THE STIRLING PRIZE
1996 Hodder Associates, University of Salford
1997 Michael Wilford & Partners, Music School, Stuttgart
1998 Foster and Partners, American Air Museum, Duxford
1999 Future Systems, NatWest Media Centre, Lord's, London
2000 Alsop & Störmer, Peckham Library, London
2001 Wilkinson Eyre Architects, Magna, Rotherham
2002 Wilkinson Eyre Architects, Millennium Bridge, Gateshead
2003 Herzog & De Meuron, Laban, Deptford, London
2004 Foster and Partners, 30 St Mary Axe, London

THE ARCHITECTS' JOURNAL FIRST BUILDING AWARD
2001 Walker Architecture, Cedar House, Logiealmond
2002 Sutherland Hussey, Barnhouse, Highgate, London
2003 De Rijke Marsh Morgan, No. 1 Centaur Street, London
2004 Annalie Riches, Silvia Ullmayer and Barti Garibaldo, In-Between, London

THE CROWN ESTATE CONSERVATION AWARD
1998 Peter Inskip and Peter Jenkins, Temple of Concord and Victory, Stowe
1999 Foster and Partners, the Reichstag, Berlin
2000 Foster and Partners, JC Decaux UK Headquarters, London
2001 Rick Mather Architects, Dulwich Picture Gallery, London

2002 Richard Murphy Architects, with Simpson Brown Architects, Stirling Tolbooth
2003 LDN Architects, Newhailes House Coservation, Musselburgh
2004 HOK International, the King's Library, The British Museum, London

THE MANSER MEDAL
2001 Cezary Bednarski, Merthyr Terrace, London
2003 Burd, Haward, Marston Architects, Brooke Coombes House, London
2003 Jamie Fobert Architects, Anderson House, London
2004 Mole Architects, The Black House, Prickwillow

THE RIBA CLIENT OF THE YEAR
1998 Roland Paoletti
1999 The MCC
2000 The Foreign and Commonwealth Office
2001 Molendinar Park Housing Association, Glasgow
2002 Urban Splash
2003 City of Manchester
2004 The Peabody Trust

THE ADAPT TRUST ACCESS AWARD
2001 Avery Associates Architects, Royal Academy of Dramatic Arts, London
2002 Malcolm Fraser Architects, Dance Base, Edinburgh
2003 Nicholl Russell Studios, The Space, Dundee College

THE RIBA INCLUSIVE DESIGN AWARD
2004   Arup Associates, City of Manchester Stadium

THE RIBA JOURNAL SUSTAINABILITY AWARD
2000   Chetwood Associates, Sainsbury's, Greenwich
2001   Michael Hopkins & Partners, Jubilee Campus, Nottingham University
2002   Cottrell + Vermeulen, Cardboard Building, Westborough School, Westcliff-on-Sea
2003   Bill Dunster Architects, BedZED, Wallington
2004   Sarah Wigglesworth Architects, Stock Orchard Street, London

THE STEPHEN LAWRENCE PRIZE
1998   Ian Ritchie Architects, Terrasson Cultural Greenhouse, France
1999   Munkenbeck + Marshall Architects, Sculpture Gallery, Roche Court, Salisbury
2000   Softroom Architects, Kielder Belvedere
2001   Richard Rose-Casemore, Hatherley Studio, Winchester
2002   Cottrell + Vermeulen, Cardboard Building, Westborough School, Westcliff-on-Sea
2003   Gumuchdjian Architects, Think Tank, Skibberreen, Ireland
2004   Simon Conder Associates, Vista, Dungeness

SPONSORS

 The RIBA is grateful to all the sponsors who make the Awards possible, in particular *The Architects' Journal*, published by EMAP, the main sponsors, who provide the money for the RIBA Stirling Prize and its judging costs. *The Architects' Journal* has been promoting good architecture since 1895. Its weekly news coverage, comprehensive building studies, in-depth technical and practice features and incisive commentary make it the UK's leading architectural magazine, whose authoritative voice has informed generations of architects.

The Architects' Journal also sponsors the AJ First Building Award in association with Robin Ellis Design & Construction. The prize is intended to mark the successful transition by a young practice from interiors and small works to a complete piece of architecture.

The RIBA would also like to thank the other sponsors of the Special Awards:

The Centre for Accessible Environments, which is an information provider and a forum for collaborative dialogue between providers and users on how the built environment can best be made or modified to achieve inclusion by design; and Allgood, which manufactures a wide range of Disability Discrimination Act compliant architectural ironmongery – joint sponsors of the RIBA Inclusive Design Award.

Arts Council England, which has sponsored The RIBA/Arts Council England Client of the Year Award from its inception in 1998. Arts Council England is the national development agency for the arts in England, distributing public money from government and the National Lottery.

The Marco Goldschmied Foundation, established by RIBA past president Marco Goldschmied, sponsors of The Stephen Lawrence Prize, established in 1998 in memory of the murdered black teenager who aspired to be an architect. Marco Goldschmied's foundation also supports the Stephen Lawrence Charitable Trust and in particular its bursary programme, which helps train black architects (www.stephenlawrence.org.uk).

The Crown Estate, sponsors of The Crown Estate Conservation Award first presented in 1998, which manages a large and uniquely diverse portfolio of land and buildings across the UK. One of its primary concerns is to make historic buildings suitable for today's users.

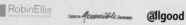

Our partners in the Manser Medal, *The Best of British Homes*, published by Emap Construct, which is an annual reference work of award-winning housing, showcasing exemplars of best design practice, and sponsor The Velux group, the world's leading supplier of roof windows, accessories and blinds.

All RIBA Award winners receive a lead plaque, produced and donated by the Lead Sheet Association, to be placed on the building. The LSA is the primary independent body involved in the promotion and development of the use of rolled-lead sheet. It offers authoritative technical advice and comprehensive training services to ensure that rolled-lead sheet maintains its matchless reputation as one of the most established long-lasting and environmentally friendly construction materials. The LSA is proud to have been associated with the RIBA Awards since 1989.

The RIBA would also like to thank the sponsors of the RIBA Stirling Prize Presentation Dinner:
Pendock, suppliers of architectural casing solutions and washroom systems;
SIV Architectural Career Management, the industry's pre-eminent recruitment service and creative business team, who co-ordinate exclusive assignments and introductions for senior-level architectural individuals and clients;
Haworth, the largest privately owned office furniture company in the world, which donated the stage furniture for the Stirling presentation;
Bentley Systems, whose software solutions enable the design, construction and operation of all types of buildings and facilities around the world.

The RIBA would also like to thank Channel 4 and TalkbackTHAMES for their continuing coverage of The RIBA Stirling Prize in association with *The Architects' Journal*.

PHOTOGRAPHERS
The RIBA would like to thank those photographers – whose work is published in this book and who are credited in the main text – who agreed to waive copyright fees for reproduction by the RIBA of their work in connection with the promotion of the RIBA Awards.

INDEX